EDITOR:
Maryanne Blacker
FRONT COVER DESIGN:
Neil Carlyle
ASSISTANT EDITOR:
Judy Newman

SUB-EDITOR:
Mary-Anne Danaher
ARTIST:
Mark Nichols
CADET ARTIST:
Louise McGeachie

PHOTOGRAPHER:
André Martin
STYLIST:
Francesca Dougall
FOOD STYLIST:
Michelle Gorry

PUBLISHER:
Richard Walsh

Produced by The Australian Women's Weekly Home Library Division. Typeset by Photoset Computer Service Pty Ltd, Sydney, Australia. Printed by Dai Nippon Co Ltd, Tokyo, Japan. Published by Australian Consolidated Press, 54 Park Street, Sydney. Distributed by Network Distribution Company, 54 Park Street, Sydney.

The Australian Women's Weekly Home Library

Fete Favourites

Fetes call for new and different ideas which can be made for little cash. This book is brimming with practical and pretty crafts; beautiful baby wear and tempting treats from the kitchen — all easy and inexpensive to make. Here's to a creative and fun fete!

For THE KITCHEN

One well-dressed breakfast set coming up! It's crocheted, and takes only a couple of balls for cosy, egg cover, pot holder and mitt. Turn the pages for more kitchen sets; some knitted, some sewn. We also show you how to make plain tea towels pretty with embroidered motifs, plus how calico and gingham can make the most appealing kitchen additions. And, our beaut beaded jug cover could well be *the* fete favourite.

RIGHT: Blue and Cream Kitchen Set (instructions overpage).

◁ BLUE AND CREAM KITCHEN SET

Note: Before commencing it is essential to first check your tension (see below)

Tea Cosy fits a 6 cup teapot

YARN REQUIREMENTS:
Villawool 8 Ply Machinewash (50g) Balls

	Cream (C)	Blue (B)
Tea Cosy	1	¼
Oven Mitt	¾	¼
Pot Holder	½	¼
Egg Cosy		Small quantity each colour

Abbreviations: See page 125. Additional abbreviations below.
Accessories: 5mm (No. 6) crochet hook or SIZE NEEDED TO GIVE CORRECT TENSION. 1 Button for Tea Cosy; Felt to back Pot Holder.
Additional Abbreviations: "Dec" = Draw up a loop in each of next 2 sts, yoh and draw through all 3 loops on hook.
Tension: 18dc and 22 rows to 10cm over dc fabric, using 5mm hook. To achieve the desired soft effect, these items have been designed to be worked on a bigger hook at a looser tension than usually recommended.

TEA COSY (make 2 pieces)
Using C, make 41ch.
1st Row: Miss 1ch, 1dc in each ch to end.
40dc.
2nd Row: 1ch, 1dc in each dc to end.
Note: When changing colours, use the new colour to draw through the last loop of the last st of the old colour.
Rep 2nd row, working 2 more rows C, then 4 rows each B, C and B.
Using C for rem, work a further 12 rows.

SHAPE TOP
29th Row: 1ch, 1dc in next dc, * "Dec", 1dc in each of next 2dc, rep from * to last 3dc, "Dec", 1dc in last dc.
30 sts.
Work 2 Rows.
32nd Row: 1ch, * "Dec", 1dc in next dc, rep from * to end.
20 sts.
Work 2 rows.
35th Row: 1ch, * "Dec", rep from * to end.
10 sts.
Work 1 row.
37th Row: As 35th row.
5 sts. Fasten off.

TO MAKE UP:
Using a flat seam, join side seams, leaving openings for spout and handle (leave seam open below handle). Join C with a sl st in top edge, make 15ch for loop, sl st in opposite edge, turn, work 24dc in loop, sl st in base of 15ch. Fasten off.
Run a thread through top edge and draw up tightly. Make a buttonloop at lower edge below handle and sew on button.

OVEN MITT
Using C, make 39ch.
1st Row: Miss 1ch, 1dc in each ch to end.
38dc.
2nd Row: 1ch, 1dc in each dc to end.
Note: When changing colours, use the new colour to draw through the last loop of the last st of the old colour.
Rep 2nd row, working 2 more rows C, then 4 rows B. Break off B.
Using C, **9th Row:** 1ch, 2dc in first dc, 1dc in each dc to last dc, 2dc in last dc.
Rep 9th row 8 times.
56dc.
Inc (as before) in foll alt row.
58dc.
Work 6 rows without shaping.
Fasten off.
Using B, **25th Row:** Miss 10dc, join yarn with a sl st in next dc, 1ch, 1dc in same place as sl st, 1dc in each of next 37dc, turn.
38dc.
Work 12 rows without shaping, working 3 more rows B, 4 rows each C and B, then 1 row C.

SHAPE TOP
Using C for rem, **38th Row:** 1ch ("Dec", 1dc in each of next 15dc, "Dec") twice.
39th and Alt Rows: 1ch, 1dc in each st to end.
40th Row: 1ch, ("Dec", 1dc in each of next 13dc, "Dec") twice.
42nd Row: 1ch, ("Dec", 1dc in each of next 11dc, "Dec") twice.
44th Row: 1ch, ("Dec", 1dc in each of next 9dc, "Dec") twice.
22 sts. Fasten off.

TO MAKE UP:
Using a flat seam, join seam. Join C with a sl st at outside edge at wrist, 15ch, sl st in next dc, turn, work 24dc in loop, sl st in base of 15ch. Fasten off.

POT HOLDER
Using C, make 5ch, join with a sl st to form ring.
1st Round: 1ch, 10dc in ring, sl st in first dc.
2nd Round: 1ch, 2dc in same place as sl st, 2dc in each dc to end, sl st in first dc.
3rd Round: 1ch, 1dc in each dc to end, sl st in first dc.
4th Round: 1ch, 1dc in same place as sl st, * 2dc in next dc, 1dc in next dc, rep from * to last dc, 2dc in last dc, sl st in first dc.
5th Round: As 3rd round, using B for sl st at end.
Using B, **6th Round:** 1ch, 1dc in same place as sl st, 1dc in next dc, * 2dc in next dc, 1dc in each of next 2dc, rep from * to last dc, 2dc in last dc, sl st in first dc.
Working in stripes of 3 more rounds B, then 4 rounds each C, B, and C, inc in this manner (working 1 more dc between inc each time) in alt rounds.
110dc.
Make 15ch for loop, sl st in next dc, turn, work 24dc in loop, sl st in base of 15ch. Fasten off.

EGG COSY
Using C, make 25ch.
1st Row: Miss 1ch, 1dc in each ch to end.
24dc.
2nd Row: 1ch, 1dc in each dc to end.
Note: When changing colours, use the new colour to draw through the last loop of the last st of the old colour.
Rep 2nd row, working 2 more rows C, then 4 rows each B and C.

SHAPE TOP:
Using B for rem, **13th Row:** 1ch, * 1dc in each of next 2dc, "Dec", rep from * to end.
14th Row: 1ch, * 1dc in next dc, "Dec", rep from * to end.
15th Row: 1ch, *"Dec", rep from * to end.
16th Row: As 15th row.
3dc.
Make 7ch for loop, sl st in centre dc, turn, work 12dc in loop, sl st in base of 7ch. Fasten off.

TO MAKE UP:
Using a flat seam, join seam.

JAM COVERS ▷

40cm gingham fabric (makes 8, we used gingham with 3mm checks)
Stranded embroidery thread (see key for colours)
Lace

Cut out a circle of gingham with a 19cm diameter or equal to the diameter of the jar being covered plus 6cm.

Work cross stitch motif in centre of the circle following graphs at right. Use four strands of thread for cross stitch and two strands for back stitch and French knots on bee.

Stitch a 5mm hem around edge of circle. Pin lace around edge, stitch.

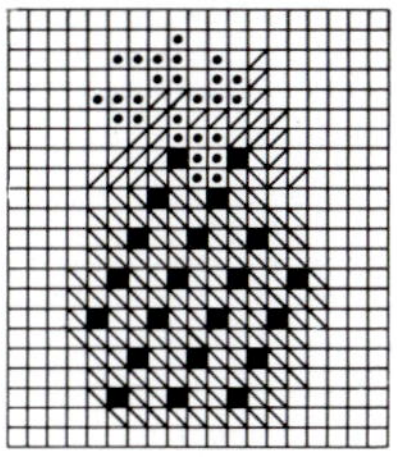

PINEAPPLE

⧅ DMC 725
■ DMC 839
⊡ DMC 704
⧄ DMC 904

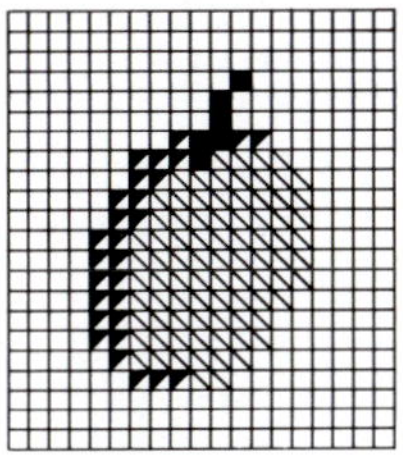

GRAPE

⧅ DMC 552
■ DMC 839
◪ DMC 550

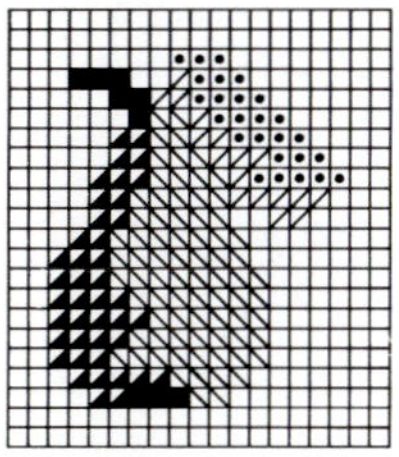

PEAR

⧅ DMC 726
◪ DMC 742
■ DMC 839
⧄ DMC 904
⊡ DMC 704

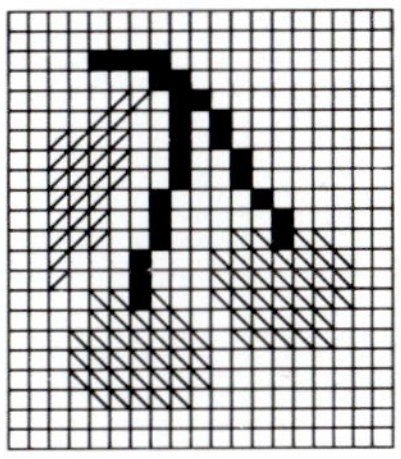

CHERRIES

⧅ DMC 326
■ DMC 839
⧄ DMC 904

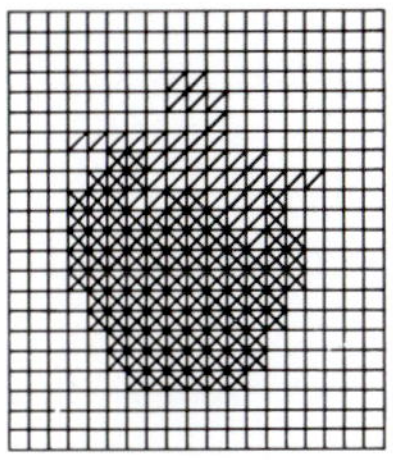

STRAWBERRY

⧄ DMC 904
⊠ DMC 321

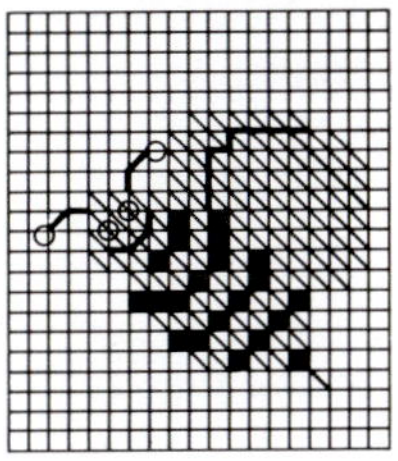

BEE

⧅ DMC 726
■ DMC 310
○ DMC 310 FRENCH KNOTS
— DMC 310 BACK STITCH

KNITTED PINEAPPLE TEA AND EGG COSIES ▽

Note: Before commencing it is essential to first check your tension (see below)

MEASUREMENTS
Tea Cosy fits a 2 Cup Teapot.

YARN REQUIREMENTS:
Villawool 8 Ply Machinewash (50g) Balls

Tea Cosy	
Main Colour (M)	1
Contrast (C)	1
Egg Cosy	Small quantity each colour

(1 ball of each colour will make Tea Cosy and 1 Egg Cosy)

Abbreviations: See page 125.
Accessories: 1 pair 4mm (No. 8) knitting needles or SIZE NEEDED TO GIVE CORRECT TENSION.
Tension: 28 sts and 28 rows to 10cm over patt, using 4mm needles.

TEA COSY (make 2 pieces)
Using M, cast on 46 sts.
1st Row (wrong side): Knit.
2nd and 4th Rows: Purl.
3rd Row: P1, * (K1, P1, K1) in front of next st, P3 tog, rep from * to last st, P1.
5th Row: P1, * P3 tog, (K1, P1, K1) in front of next st, rep from * to last st, P1.
Rows 2 to 5 incl form patt.
Cont in patt until work measures 14cm from beg, ending with a 5th row.
Next Row: P1, * K1, P3 tog, rep from * to last st, P1.
24 sts.
Next Row: * P2 tog, rep from * to end.
12 sts.
Cast off.

INNER LEAVES
Using C, cast on 45 sts.
* **1st Row:** (K1, P1) 4 times, K1, turn.
Cont on these 9 sts.
2nd Row: K2, (P1, K1) 3 times, K1.
Rep 1st and 2nd rows 7 times.
17th Row: (K1, P3 tog) twice, K1.
18th Row: K2, P1, K2.
19th Row: K1, P3 tog, K1.
20th Row: K3.
21st Row: P3 tog. Fasten off. *
(Join yarn to rem sts, rep from * to *) 4 times.

OUTER LEAVES
Work as for Inner Leaves, but rep 1st and 2nd rows 5 times instead of 7 times.

TO MAKE UP:
Do not press. Using back stitch, join side seams, leaving an opening for handle and spout. Join ends of cast-on edges of leaves to form a ring. Sew 2 sets of leaves tog, then gather up firmly and sew to top of cosy, gathering top of cosy if necessary.

EGG COSY
Using M, cast on 38 sts.
1st Row (wrong side): Knit.
Work rows 2 to 5 incl as for Tea Cosy 4 times.
Next Row: P1, * K1, P3 tog, rep from * to last st, P1.
20 sts.
Next Row: * P2 tog, rep from * to end.
10 sts.
Cast off.

INNER LEAVES
Using C, cast on 25 sts.
* **1st Row:** (K1, P1) twice, K1, turn.
Cont on these 5 sts.
2nd Row: K2, P1, K2.
Rep 1st and 2nd rows 3 times.
9th Row: K1, P3 tog, K1.
10th Row: K3.
11th Row: P3 tog. Fasten off. *
(Join yarn to rem sts, rep from * to *) 4 times.

OUTER LEAVES
Work as for Inner Leaves, but rep 1st and 2nd rows twice instead of 3 times.

TO MAKE UP:
Do not press. Using back stitch, join side seam. Join ends of cast-on edges of leaves to form a ring. Sew 2 sets of leaves tog, then gather up firmly and sew to top of cosy, gathering top of cosy if necessary.

OVEN MITT WITH BEETROOT MOTIF ▷

30cm calico
Stranded embroidery thread in green and deep purple
Bias binding
Felt for padding
20 × 15cm waste canvas

Cut fabric and padding using pattern for Oranges and Lemons Set Oven Mitt on page 10. Tack waste canvas to one piece calico.

Embroider calico with waste canvas using design from graph below in cross stitch and two strands of thread. Use green thread for leaves and purple for beetroot. See 126 for stitch instructions. Remove waste canvas threads.

Place together two padding pieces between wrong sides of two mitt fabric pieces, for one side of mitt. Repeat for other side of mitt. Tack both sides mitt together and bind outside edge with bias binding, ending with a loop to hang mitt. Bind wrist edge with bias binding.

Mitt by Robyn Birkenshaw

Beetroot pot mit

DMC 991 ☒
DMC 915 ⧅

SPICE ROPE ▽

2m narrow ribbon
3m thin rope
Fabric scraps
2 cinnamon sticks
Cloves
Anise
Nutmeg

Cut three pieces of fabric 10cm x 20cm. Hem short ends, fold in half, right sides together and stitch up sides, so hem is at top. Turn right side out to form a small pouch. Fill each pouch with spice.

Cut rope into three 1m lengths. Plait rope and tie a knot at each end. Tie spice bags and cinnamon sticks to rope with ribbon.

Spice rope by Susan Massey

PRESERVE COVERS ▽

Note: Before commencing it is essential to first check your tension (see below)

MEASUREMENTS			
Size		Large	Small
Diameter (approx)	CM	28	20
	INS	11	8
YARN REQUIREMENTS:			
Patons Gem 4 Ply (50g) Ball		¾	½

Abbreviations: See page 125.
Additional abbreviations below.
Accessories: 1 set 2.75mm (No. 12) knitting needles or SIZE NEEDED TO GIVE CORRECT TENSION.
Additional Abbreviations: "M2" = (K1, P1) into front of next st; "M3" = (K1, P1, K1) into front of next st.
Tension: 29 sts and 38.5 rows to 10cm over stocking st, using 2.75mm needles.

LARGE PRESERVE COVER (beg at centre)
Cast on 8 sts (3,3,2). Join into a round, taking care not to twist cast-on edge.
1st Round: Knit.
2nd Round: * Y fwd, K1, rep from * to end.
16 sts.
Knit 3 rounds.
6th Round: As 2nd round.
32 sts.
Knit 3 rounds.
10th Round: K1, * y fwd, K2, rep from * to last st, y fwd, K1.
48 sts.
11th Round: K1, * "M2", K2, rep from * to last 2 sts, "M2", K1.
64 sts.
12th Round: * K2 tog, y fwd, sl 1, K1, psso, rep from * to end.
48 sts.
Rep 11th and 12th rounds 4 times.
21st Round: K1, * "M3", K2, rep from * to last 2 sts, "M3", K1.
80 sts.
Knit 3 rounds.
25th Round: * Y fwd, K5, rep from * to end.
96 sts.
26th and Alt Rounds: Knit. **
27th Round: * Inc in next st, y fwd, sl 1, K1, psso, K1, K2 tog, y fwd, rep from * to end, then knit first st of round on to end of last needle (thus moving end of round — this will now be referred to as "knit first st").
112 sts.
29th Round: K2, * y fwd, sl 1, K2 tog, psso, y fwd, K4, rep from *, ending last rep with K2 instead of K4.
31st Round: * Y fwd, K7, rep from * to end.
128 sts.
33rd Round: * Inc in next st, y fwd, sl 1, K1, psso, K3, K2 tog, y fwd, rep from * to end, "knit first st".
144 sts.
35th Round: K2, * y fwd, sl 1, K1, psso, K1, K2 tog, y fwd, K4, rep from * ending last rep with K2 instead of K4.
37th Round: * Y fwd, K3, y fwd, sl 1, K2 tog, psso, y fwd, K3, rep from * to end.
160 sts.
39th Round: * K1, y fwd, sl 1, K1, psso, K5, K2 tog, y fwd, rep from * to end.
41st Round: * Y fwd, K2 tog, y fwd, sl 1, K1, psso, K3, K2 tog, y fwd, K1, rep from * to end.
43rd Round: * Sl 1, K1, psso, y fwd, K1, y fwd, sl 1, K1, psso, K1, K2 tog, y fwd, sl 1, K1, psso, y fwd, rep from * to end.
45th Round: * (Y fwd, K2 tog) twice, y fwd, sl 1, K2 tog, psso, y fwd, K1, y fwd, K2 tog, rep from * to end.
***** 47th Round:** * Sl 1, K1, psso, y fwd, rep from * to end.
48th Round: Knit.
49th Round: * Y fwd, K2 tog, rep from * to end.
50th Round: Knit.
Insert needle into next st and cast on 8 sts for **Edging**.
1st Row: K8, turn.
2nd Row: Sl 1, K2, y fwd, K2 tog, (y fwd) twice, K2 tog, K1.
3rd Row: K3, P1, K2, y fwd, (K2 tog) twice (last K2 tog uses one st of edging and one st of centre), turn.
4th Row: Sl 1, K2, y fwd, K2 tog, K1, (y fwd) twice, K2 tog, K1.
5th Row: K3, P1, K3, y fwd, (K2 tog) twice, turn.
6th Row: Sl 1, K2, y fwd, K2 tog, K2, (y fwd) twice, K2 tog, K1.
7th Row: K3, P1, K4, y fwd, (K2 tog) twice, turn.
8th Row: Sl 1, K2, y fwd, K2 tog, K6.

9th Row: Cast off 3 sts, K5, y fwd, (K2 tog) twice, turn.
Rep rows 2 to 9 incl until all centre sts have been worked off. Cast off.

SMALL PRESERVE COVER
Work as for Large Preserve Cover to **.
27th Round: * K1, y fwd, sl 1, K1, psso, K1, K2 tog, y fwd, rep from * to end.
29th Round: * Y fwd, K2 tog, y fwd, sl 1, K2 tog, psso, y fwd, K1, rep from * to end.
30th Round: Knit.
Complete as for Large Preserve Cover from *** to end.

TO MAKE UP:
Using a flat seam, join cast-on and cast-off edges of edging. With a slightly damp cloth and warm iron, press lightly.

BELOW: From left: Preserve Cover with Star Motif; Preserve Cover (small and large).

▽PRESERVE COVER WITH STAR MOTIF

Note: Before commencing it is essential to first check your tension (see below)

MEASUREMENTS		
Diameter (approx)	CM	23
	INS	9

YARN REQUIREMENTS:	
Patons Gem 4 Ply (50g) Balls	⅓

Abbreviations: See page 125.
Additional abbreviations below.
Accessories: 1 set 2.75mm (No. 12) knitting needles or SIZE NEEDED TO GIVE CORRECT TENSION.
Additional Abbreviations: "M2" = (y fwd) twice (thus making 2 sts).
Tension: 29 sts and 38.5 rows to 10cm over stocking st, using 2.75mm needles.

PRESERVE COVER (beg at centre)
Cast on 6 sts (2,2,2). Join into a round, taking care not to twist cast-on edge.
1st and Alt Rounds to 15th Round: Knit.
2nd Round: * Y fwd, K1, rep from * to end.
4th Round: * Y fwd, K2, rep from * to end.
6th Round: * Y fwd, K3, rep from * to end.
8th Round: * Y fwd, K4, rep from * to end.
10th Round: * Y fwd, K5, rep from * to end.
12th Round: * Y fwd, K6, rep from * to end.
14th Round: * Y fwd, K7, rep from * to end.
16th Round: * Y fwd, K8, rep from * to end.
17th Round: * K1, y fwd, sl 1, K1, psso, K6, rep from * to end.
18th Round: * Y fwd, K9, rep from * to end.
19th Round: * K1, y fwd, K2 tog, y fwd, sl 1, K1, psso, K5, rep from * to end.
20th Round: * Y fwd, K10, rep from * to end.
21st Round: * K1, (y fwd, K2 tog) twice, y fwd, sl 1, K1, psso, K4, rep from * to end.
22nd Round: * Y fwd, K11, rep from * to end.
23rd Round: * K1, (y fwd, K2 tog) 3 times, y fwd, sl 1, K1, psso, K3, rep from * to end.
24th Round: * Y fwd, K12, rep from * to end.
25th Round: * K1, (y fwd, K2 tog) 4 times, y fwd, sl 1, K1, psso, K2, rep from * to end.
26th Round: * Y fwd, K13, rep from * to end.
27th Round: * K1, (y fwd, K2 tog) 5 times, y fwd, sl 1, K1, psso, K1, rep from * to end.
28th Round: * Y fwd, K14, rep from * to end.
29th Round: * K1, (y fwd, K2 tog) 6 times, y fwd, sl 1, K1, psso, rep from * to end.
30th Round: * Y fwd, K15, rep from * to end.
96 sts.
31st Round: Knit first st of round on to end of last needle, * Y fwd, K2 tog, rep from * to end.
32nd Round: Knit.
Rep 31st and 32nd rounds once.
Insert needle into next st and cast on 7 sts for **Edging**.
1st Row: K7, turn.
2nd Row: Sl 1, K2, y fwd, K2 tog,

"M2", K2.
3rd Row: K3, P1, K2, y fwd, (K2 tog) twice (last K2 tog uses one st of edging and one st of centre), turn.
4th Row: Sl 1, K2, y fwd, K2 tog, knit to end.
5th Row: K6, y fwd, (K2 tog) twice, turn.
6th Row: Sl 1, K2, y fwd, K2 tog, "M2", K2 tog, "M2", K2.
7th Row: K3, (P1, K2) twice, y fwd, (K2 tog) twice, turn.
8th Row: As 4th row.
9th Row: K9, y fwd, (K2 tog) twice, turn.
10th Row: Sl 1, K2, y fwd, K2 tog, ("M2", K2 tog) 3 times, K1.
11th Row: K3, (P1, K2) 3 times, y fwd, (K2 tog) twice, turn.
12th Row: As 4th row.
13th Row: Cast off 8 sts, K4, y fwd, (K2 tog) twice, turn.
Rep rows 2 to 13 incl until all centre sts have been worked off. Cast off.
TO MAKE UP:
Using a flat seam, join cast-on and cast-off edges of edging. With a slightly damp cloth and warm iron, press lightly.

TOOTHPICK HOLDER ▽

Heavy cardboard
Fabric scrap
30cm lace or braid
Dried or fabric flowers (if desired)
Craft glue
Small magnet

Cut two circles (9cm diameter) or two rectangles (9cm x 6.5cm). Cover both pieces cardboard with fabric by gluing it in place.

Cut a piece of fabric to form pocket. Turn top edge in and glue edges to back of one covered cardboard piece.

Glue lace around edges of one covered cardboard piece. Join front and back pieces together so pocket is facing outwards.

Glue magnet to back of holder and decorate with braid, lace or flowers.

ORANGES AND LEMONS SET ▷

60cm x 122cm fabric
50cm x 137cm felt (padding)
Bias binding

Enlarge pattern from graph below referring to page 125 for method. Cut fabric using pattern.

Oven Cloth. Place two padding layers between wrong sides of two main pieces. Fold pocket sections along foldline on pattern, right sides out, and position and tack one at each end of the main piece. Tack around edges. Stitch bias binding around edge of cloth.

Oven Mitt. Place together two padding pieces between wrong sides of two mitt fabric pieces, for one side of mitt. Repeat for other side of mitt. Bind across each straight wrist edge with bias binding. Tack both sides of mitt together and bind outside edge with bias binding, ending with a loop to hang mitt.

Pot Holder. Place three felt padding layers between wrong side of two fabric pieces. Tack together and bind edge with bias binding, ending with a loop to hang the pot holder.

Toothpick holders by Neryl Hogan

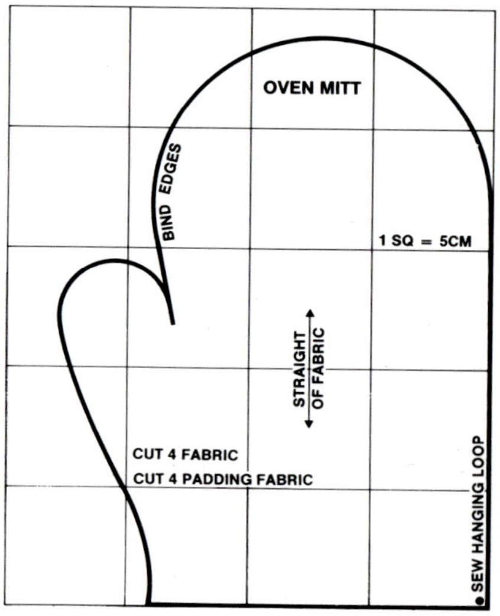

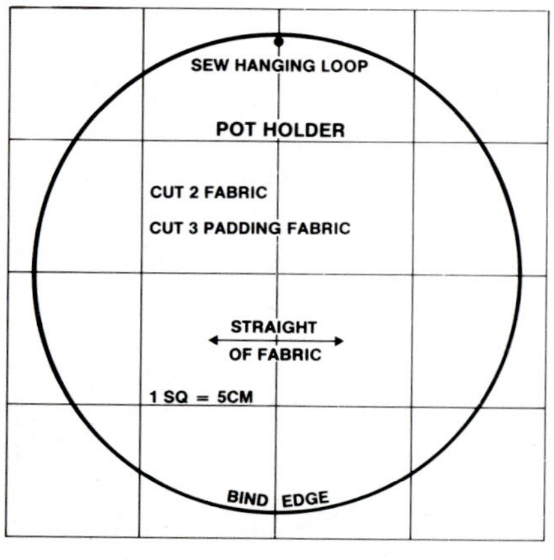

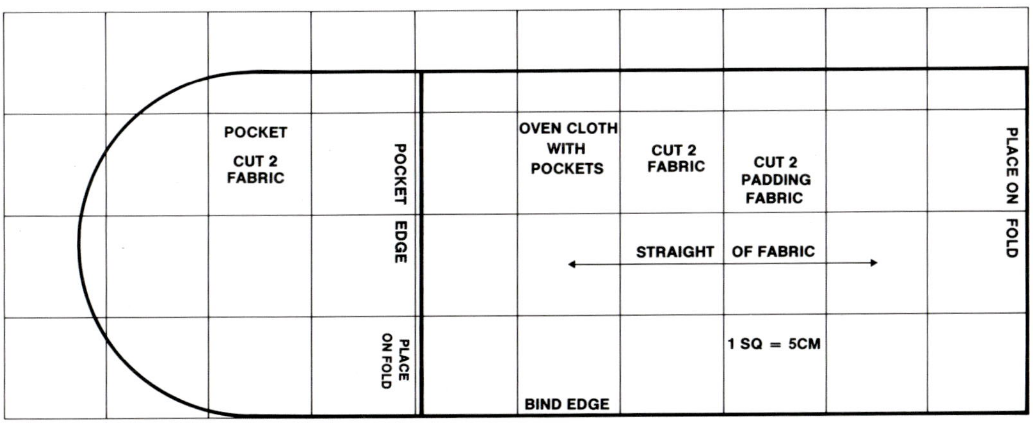

Basket from the Woollahra Galleries, N.S.W.

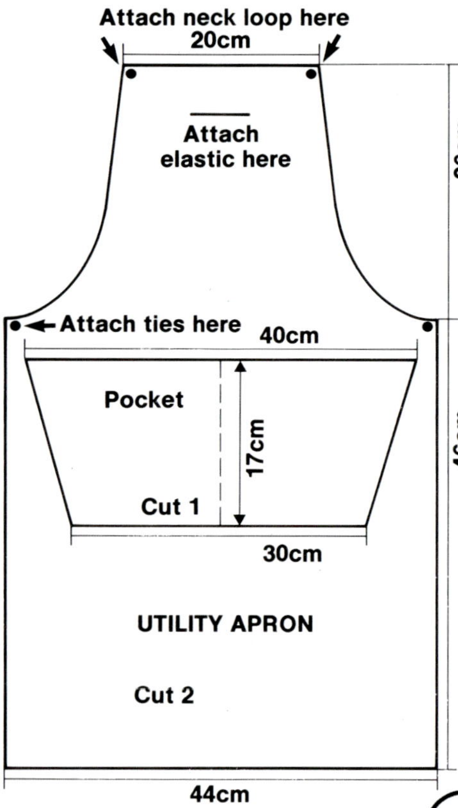

UTILITY APRON ▷

2m cotton fabric
1.9m cotton tape
50cm x 13mm elastic
Fabric paint

Trace pattern onto doubled fabric and cut out leaving 2cm extra for seams. Stitch together, leaving 20cm gap for turning out (if material is patterned stitch together with wrong sides out), turn right side out. Iron seams flat and top stitch about 5mm from edge.

Position pocket as shown on diagram, turn edges under and stitch. Divide pocket in two with a line of stitching. Loop elastic on centre panel and stitch in place; make about four loops for holding cleaning cloths, pen, scissors etc.

Trace design onto apron across bottom and front panel. Paint and add words as desired using fabric paint.

Cut cotton tape into two 60cm pieces and one 70cm piece. Stitch the 60cm pieces to sides of apron for ties and stitch ends of 70cm section to either side of the top edge for neck loop.

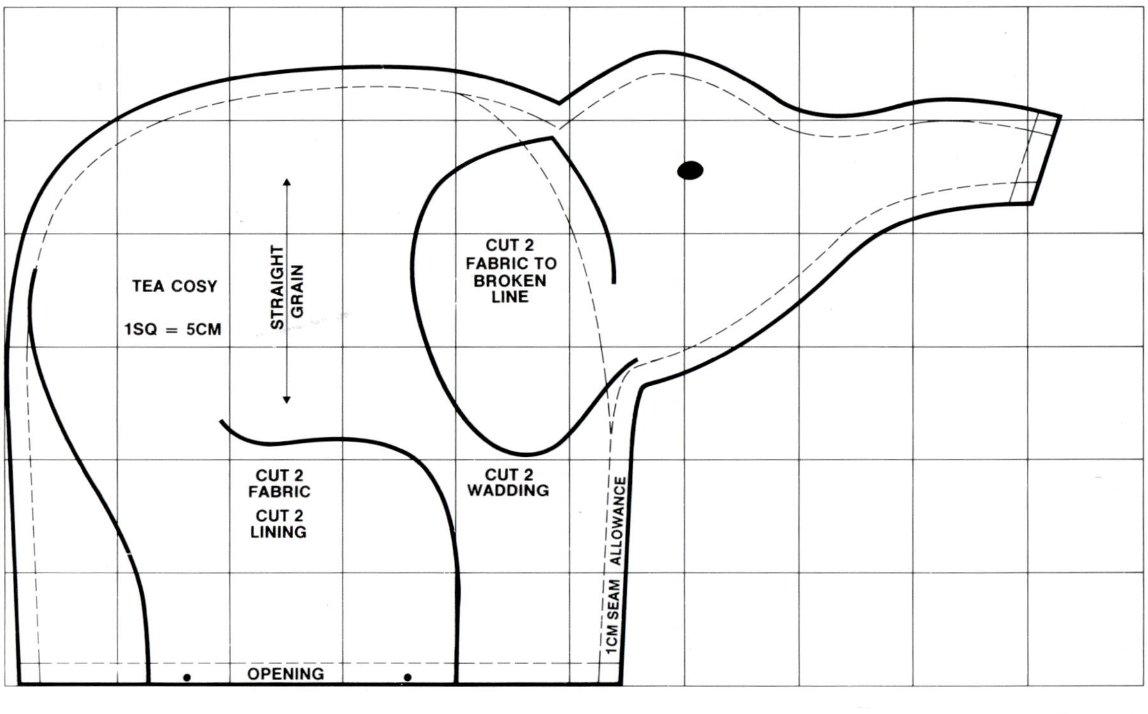

RIGHT: Tea set from Dasch

Apron by Jillian Morrow

Cosy and pot holder by Betty Smith

ELEPHANT TEA COSY AND POT HOLDER ▽

60cm x 120cm fabric
30cm x 90cm lining
30cm x 90cm polyester wadding
20cm x 90cm felt
2 wooden beads for eyes
10cm bias binding
Stranded embroidery thread

Enlarge pattern (see page 125) from graphs. Cut out fabric.

Cosy. Pin wadding and one lining to the wrong side of each fabric piece. Tack together. Using close zigzag, stitch outlines of legs and ears to each section.

With right sides together, pin and sew sides together leaving lower edge open.

Clip curves and corners, turn to right side and press seam open.

With right sides together, pin fabric cut to broken line together and sew seam leaving lower edge unsewn.

With right sides together, pin and sew this lining over outside elephant, along lower seam leaving seam open on one side as indicated between dots. Turn out, sew opening closed. Push fabric up inside cosy. Sew wooden beads in eye position.

Pot Holder. Pin and tack fabric, right sides out, to each side of two or three layers of felt padding. Sew outlines of legs and ears with close zigzag stitch. Make a loop of bias binding and place at tail position. Sew around edge of elephant with close zigzag stitch twice.

Embroider eyes using three strands of embroidery thread and satin stitch. See page 126 for stitch instructions.

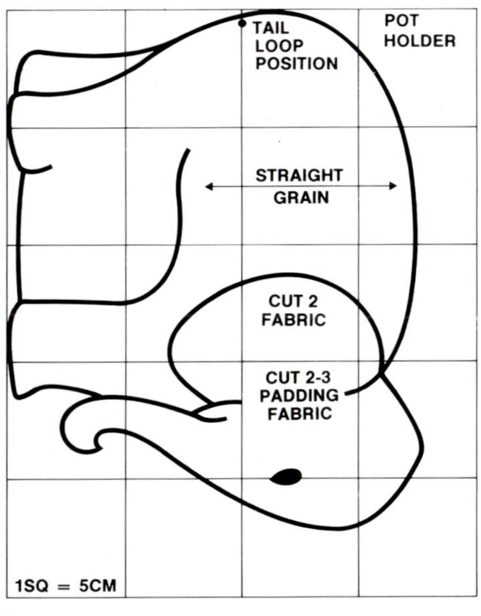

◁ FRUIT TEA TOWEL

1 tea towel
Stranded embroidery thread in the following colours: Dark plum; light plum; red; dark green; emerald

Centre design along one short edge of tea towel and trace design from diagram at right.

Work using three strands red thread for cherries, two strands dark green for stems, three strands dark and light plum for plum, three strands emerald for leaves, and two strands dark green for veins.

Work areas marked 1 in stem stitch and 2 in long and short satin stitch. See page 126 for embroidery stitch instructions.

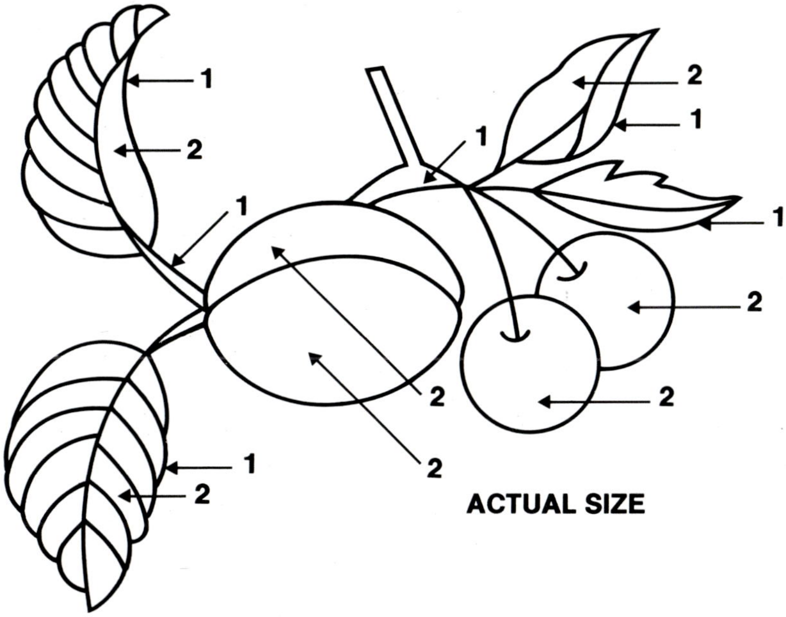

ACTUAL SIZE

STRAWBERRY TEA COSY AND POT HOLDER ▽

Note: Before commencing it is essential to first check your tension (see below)

Tea Cosy fits a 4 cup teapot.

YARN REQUIREMENTS:
Villawool 5 Ply Machinewash (50g) Balls

	Tea Cosy	Pot Holder
Red	1	1
Green	Small quantity for each	
White	Small quantity for embroidery	

Abbreviations: See page 125. Additional abbreviations below.
Accessories: 4.50mm (No. 7) crochet hook or SIZE NEEDED TO GIVE CORRECT TENSION.
1 button for Tea Cosy; felt to pad Pot Holder.
Additional Abbreviations: "Dec" = Yoh, draw up a loop in each of next 2 sts, yoh and draw through all 4 loops on hook.
Tension: 18.5htr and 16 rows to 10cm over htr fabric, using 4.50mm hook. If less sts use a smaller hook, if more sts use a bigger hook. To achieve the desired soft effect, these

items have been designed to be worked on a bigger hook at a looser tension than usually recommended.

TEA COSY (make 2 pieces)
Using red, make 36ch.
1st Row: Miss 2ch, 1htr in each ch to end.
34htr.
2nd Row: 2ch, 1htr in each htr to end.
Rep 2nd row until work measures 10cm from beg, working last row on wrong side.

SHAPE TOP:
1st Row: 2ch, 1htr in each of next 2htr, * "Dec", 1htr in each of next 2htr, rep from * to end.
26 sts.
2nd Row: 2ch, 1htr in each st to end.
3rd Row: 2ch, "Dec", * 1htr in next htr, "Dec", rep from * to end.
17 sts.
Rep 2nd and 3rd rows twice.
7sts.
Fasten off.

LEAVES
Using green, make 15ch.
1st Row: Miss 1ch, 1dc in each of next 2ch, 1htr in each of next 2ch, 1tr in each of next 2ch, 1dtr in each of next 4ch, 1tr in next ch, 1htr in next ch, 1dc in each of last 2ch.
2nd Row: 1ch, 1dc in each of first 2dc, 1htr in next htr, 1tr in next tr, 1dtr in each of next 4dtr, 1tr in each of next 2tr, 1htr in each of next 2htr, 1dc in each of last 2dc.
3rd Row: Sl st in first dc, 1dc in next dc, 1htr in each of next 2htr , 1tr in each of next 2tr, 1dtr in each of next 4dtr, 1tr in next tr, 1htr in next htr, 1dc in each of last 2dc.
4th Row: 1ch, 1dc in each of first 4 sts, turn.
5th Row: 11ch, miss 1 of these ch, 1dc in each of next 2ch, 1htr in each of next 2ch, 1tr in each of next 2ch, 1dtr in each of next 4ch, 1tr in next dc, 1htr in next dc, 1dc in each of last 2dc. **
Rep rows 2 to 5 incl 4 times, then 2nd and 3rd rows once. Do not turn.
Next Row: 1ch, working along top edge of leaves work 1dc in end of each row, join with a sl st in 1ch.
24dc, counting 1ch as 1dc.
Next Row: 1ch, * miss 1dc, 1dc in next dc, rep from * to last dc, miss last dc, sl st in 1ch at beg.
12dc.
Rep last row once.
6dc.
Make 15ch for loop, miss 2dc, sl st in next dc, turn, work 24dc in loop, sl st in base of 15ch. Fasten off.

TO MAKE UP:
Using white double, embroider spots as illustrated (for each spot, make 4 straight stitches over 2 rows). Using a flat seam, join side seams, leaving openings for spout and handle (leave seam open below handle). Join first and last leaves tog for 4 sts, then sew leaves to centre of cosy as pictured. Make a button-loop at lower edge below handle and sew on button.

POT HOLDER
Using red, make 14ch.
1st Row: Miss 2ch, 1htr in each ch to end.
12htr.
2nd Row: 2ch, 2htr in first htr, 1htr in each htr to last htr, 2htr in last htr.
Inc in this manner at each end of every row until there are 28htr, then in alt rows until there are 40htr.
Work 7 rows without shaping.
Next Row: 2ch, "Dec", 1htr in each htr to last 2htr, "Dec".
Rep last row 5 times.
28 sts.
Next Row: Sl st across first 3 sts, 1dc in each of next 3 sts, 1htr in each of next 16 sts, 1dc in each of next 3 sts, sl st across last 3 sts.
Fasten off.

LEAVES
Work as for Leaves of Tea Cosy to **.
Rep rows 2 to 5 incl twice, then 2nd and 3rd rows once. Do not turn.
Next Row: 1ch, working along top edge of leaves work 1dc in end of each row.
15dc.
Next Row: 1ch, 1dc in first dc, * miss 1dc, 1dc in next dc, rep from * to end.
8dc.
Next Row: 1ch, * miss 1dc, 1dc in next dc, rep from * to end.
4dc.
Rep last row once.
2dc.
Make 15ch for loop, miss 1dc, sl st in next dc, turn, work 24dc in loop, sl st in base of 15ch. Fasten off.

TO MAKE UP:
Embroider spots as for Tea Cosy. Sew leaves in position as pictured. Cut a piece of felt the same size as pot holder and sew to back.

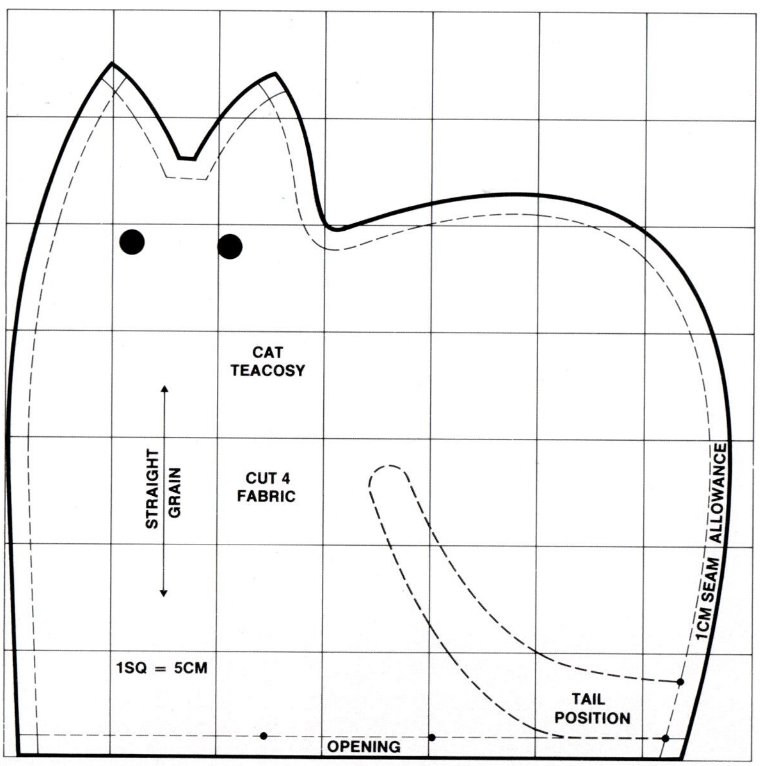

CAT TEA COSY AND POT HOLDER

60cm x 122cm fabric
40cm x 90cm polyester wadding
20cm x 90cm felt
2 buttons
Bias binding

Enlarge pattern (see page 125). Cut fabric using pattern. Cut bias strip for Cosy cat's tail, 22cm x 9cm.
Cosy. Pin and tack wadding to wrong side of two cat shapes of cosy. Pin and sew pieces together leaving lower seam unsewn. Clip curves and corners, turn out.

With right sides of fabric together fold tail strip in half along 22cm length and sew seam, rounding seam off at one end. Turn out, fill with wadding.

Pin to front side of cat and sew end with seam. Pin and sew remaining two cat shapes together sewing a wider seam and leaving

lower edges free. Clip curves and corners.

With right sides of fabric together place one over the other, pin and sew lower seam leaving opening between dots on one side. Turn out through opening. Push fabric up inside cosy. Sew opening closed. Sew on buttons for eyes, sew tail in place.

Pot Holder. Place fabric right side out on either side of two or three layers of felt padding fabric. Tack together to hold.

Sew along stitch line for face outline. Sew bias binding around outside edge using zigzag stitch and making a loop for hanging.

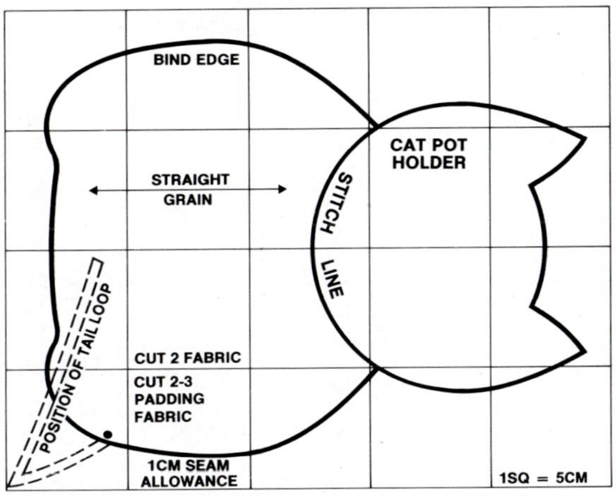

1 SQ = 1cm

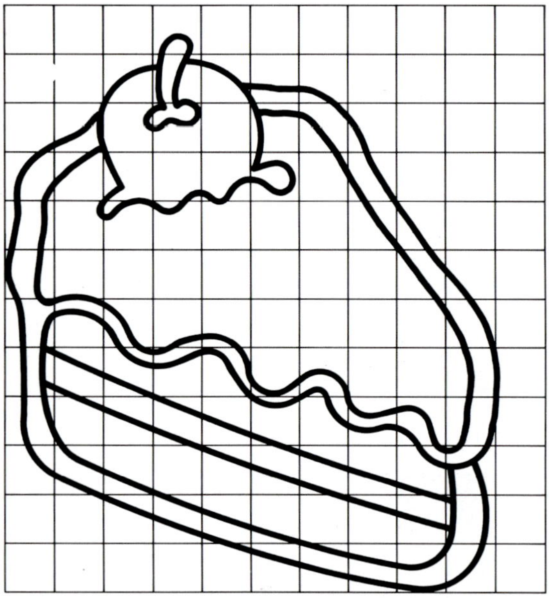

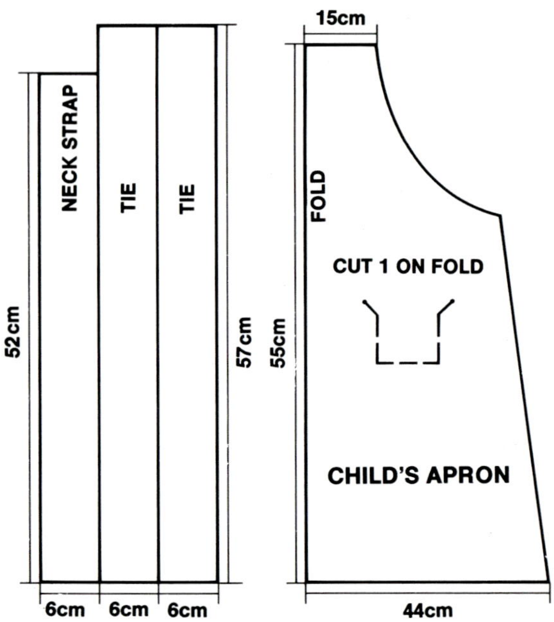

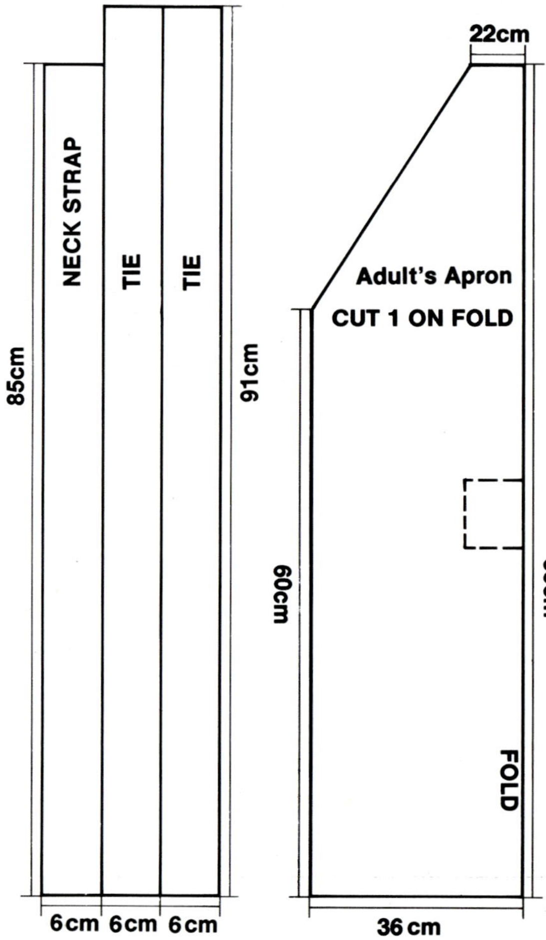

Aprons on this page by Rosa Alonso

◁ APPLIQUED APRONS ▽

1m calico (child's apron)
1.5m calico (adult's apron)
Fabric scraps (for applique)
Bias (optional)

Cut fabric from pattern. Stitch hems around long edges of ties and neck straps of apron. Press under hem all around apron. Stitch one raw edge of ties under apron hem at sides. Stitch raw edges of neck strap under hem at neck of apron.

Press strap and ties towards folded edges. Top stitch around apron. Cut applique shapes using diagrams on page opposite in fabric and colours as desired. Position shapes on apron and pocket (as pictured) and machine satin stitch around edges of appliques.

Position pocket on right side of apron turning under hem. Stitch around sides and bottom between dots. If using bias trim stitch this around pocket edge. Double stitch where ties join apron. Stitch a hem on top edge of pocket.

NB. Make button and buttonhole closure at one end of neck strap on child's apron. We left some of the bumble bee's wings free from apron fabric by satin stitching around them before stitching onto apron.

BEADED JUG COVER △

Note: Before commencing it is essential to first check your tension (see below)

MEASUREMENTS		
Size		
Diameter (approx)	CM	25
	INS	10
YARN REQUIREMENTS:		
Patons Gem 4 Ply (50g) Balls		¼

Abbreviations: See page 125.
Accessories: 3mm (No. 10-11) crochet hook or SIZE NEEDED TO GIVE CORRECT TENSION.
24 beads with large holes.
Tension: 23.5tr and 12 rows to 10cm over treble fabric, using 3mm Hook.

JUG COVER

Before beg, thread beads onto yarn (they slide along as you work).
Make 6ch, join with a sl st to form ring.
1st Round: 3ch, 15tr in ring, sl st in 3rd ch at beg.
2nd Round: 3ch, 1tr in same place as sl st, 2tr in each tr to end, sl st in 3rd ch at beg.
32tr, counting 3ch as 1tr.
3rd Round: 1dc in same place as sl st, * 3ch, miss 1tr, 1dc in next tr, rep from * to last tr, 3ch, miss 1tr, sl st in first dc.
16 loops.
4th and 5th Rounds: Sl st to centre of first loop, 1dc in same loop, * 4ch, 1dc in next loop, rep from * to end, 4 ch, sl st in first dc.
6th Round: As 4th round but working 5ch loops instead of 4ch.
7th Round: Sl st to centre of first loop, 1dc in same loop, *5ch, (1dc, 5ch, 1dc) in next loop, 5ch, 1dc in next loop, rep from * omitting 1dc at end of last rep, sl st in first dc.
24 loops.
8th and 9th Rounds: As 6th round.
10th, 11th and 12th Rounds: As 4th round but working 6ch loops instead of 4ch.
13th Round: 13ch, draw up loop on hook, remove from hook and thread it into a needle, slide a bead up to work and over needle (thus threading bead on to ch), return loop to hook and tighten, 1dc in next 6ch loop, rep from * omitting 1dc at end of last rep, sl st in first dc.
Fasten off.
With a slightly damp cloth and warm iron, press lightly.

For THE BEDROOM

Everyone loves lacy luxuries which not only look good but add a lovely fragrance to the bedroom. Make a basketful of these potpourri sachets in a variety of scents. Or try your hand at picture frames, tissue boxes and a mirror; all easily made using craft glue. Children will love their own name plaque for the bedroom door which could be made in pretty pastels or bright primary colours.

Heart Potpourri by Neryl Hogan

RIGHT: Heart Potpourri (instructions overpage).

Jumper by Weiss Pringle

Tissue box cover by Neryl Hogan

◁HEART POTPOURRI

50cm x 10cm scalloped lace
30cm pipe cleaner
Potpourri
30cm ribbon
Craft glue
Dried flowers

Cut 40cm piece lace, make 3cm casing along straight edge of lace by folding and stitching along one side. Push pipe cleaner through casing and join ends by twisting together and pushing lace over join.

Form pipe cleaner into shape required e.g. heart or circle. Glue ends of lace neatly under to form hem at back of ring.

To make potpourri bag fold 10cm lace in half, wrong sides together and glue along edges. Turn to right side.

Fill with potpourri and tie ribbon around bag neck.

Glue potpourri bag to wrong side of heart shape. Glue a loop of ribbon in place at top of shape for hanging. Decorate by gluing dried flowers onto bag.

△TISSUE BOX COVER

Heavy cardboard
Wadding
50cm fabric
Braid
Lace
Craft glue

To cover any sized tissue box first measure top of box and transfer measurements to sheet of heavy cardboard, (piece 1 on diagram).

Measure sides and draw as an addition to box top on cardboard. (Pieces 2, 3, 4 and 5)

Measure halfway along pieces 5 and 3 and add this width to the sides of 2 and 4. Cut out around outline.

With sharp knife or scissors, score along lines A-B, C-D, E-F, G-H. Cut along both sides of 5 and 3 to 1. (These half pieces form flaps to fold underneath when making box.

Cut hole in top of box; it can be circular, oval, square or any shape you desire.

Cover all areas, except flaps, with wadding. Cover with fabric, cutting fabric 1cm larger than pattern to allow for turning under. Let fabric lap over 1cm on to flaps.

Fold flaps inwards and glue together. Glue sides of box over flaps and hold in place with pegs or sticky tape until firm.

Glue braid and lace around box and opening to decorate box.

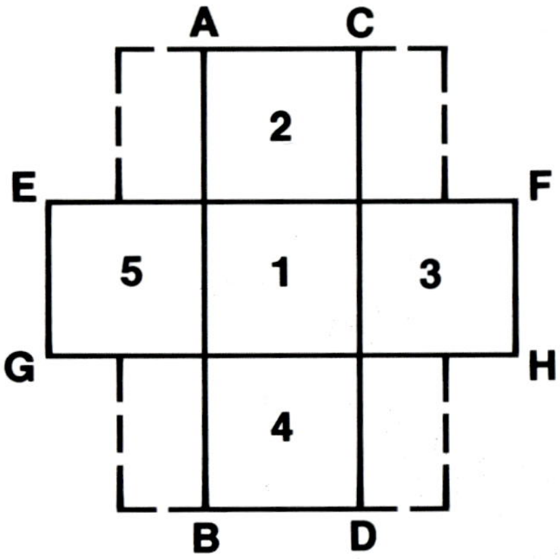

COVERED MIRROR▷

Round mirror, 14cm diameter
Heavy cardboard
Ice cream stick
Polyester wadding
50cm fabric
Braid
Dried flowers
Craft glue
Ribbon bow

Cut two shapes from heavy cardboard using pattern on page at right. One piece (front piece) has hole cut in it for the mirror (should be a little smaller than mirror).

Glue wadding to both pieces then cover them with fabric, gluing allowances to underside of cardboard.

On piece with hole for mirror, cut out fabric for hole leaving 3cm to be snipped back to cardboard edge and turned under then glued to underside.

Reinforce cardboard handle by gluing an ice cream stick vertically along the handle on the back of one piece.

If using braid to trim mirror, glue to inner edge of mirror hole. Place the two fabric covered pieces together but do not glue. Mark mirror hole on back piece and then glue mirror to back piece.

Glue two pieces together and hold in place with pegs until stuck.

Squeeze outer edges of frame occasionally while drying. Be careful not to press hard and break glass.

Once glue is dry, glue braid to outer edges. Finish by decorating with a ribbon bow and flowers.

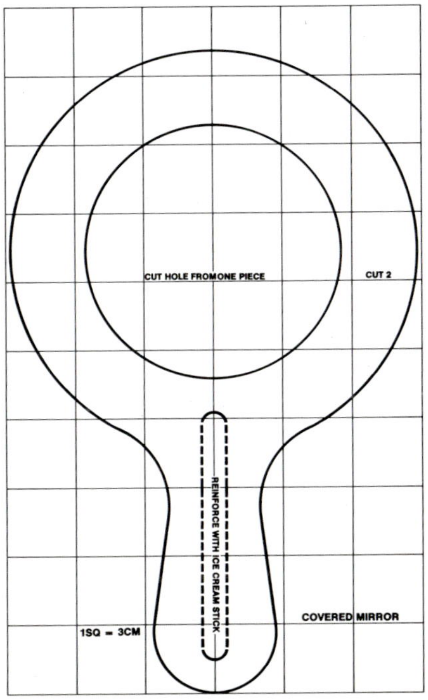

ROUND LINED CANE BASKET ▽

Round cane basket
Fabric scrap
Thin cardboard
Lace
Ribbon
Craft glue

Cut circle of cardboard slightly smaller than inside base of basket. Cover with fabric.

Measure around circumference of basket, and width of basket wall. Cut piece fabric 2cm larger than width and length.

Glue fabric around inside of basket wall turning under edges. Insert base into basket (may be glued).

Trim outside of box with lace, ribbon and dried flowers, as desired.

SMALL ROUND JEWELLERY BOX ▽

Heavy cardboard tube (8cm diameter, 4cm height)
Circle heavy cardboard for base (8cm diameter)
Circle light cardboard for inside base (6cm diameter)
2 circles light cardboard for lid (7.5cm diameter)
Fabric scrap
50cm braid
30cm lace
Ribbon roses
Craft glue

Cut fabric pieces using cardboard as a pattern and adding allowances.

Cover tube with fabric outside, then inside. Inside covering may lap over top and be glued on outside then covered with lace and braid. ▷

Mirror, box and basket by Neryl Hogan

Cover base with fabric. Glue tube to base. Cover inside base with fabric then glue into bottom of box.

Cover two lid sections with fabric and glue together.

Glue braid around lid and bottom of box. Glue lace then braid around top edge of box.

Decorate lid with ribbon roses and braid as desired.

TRIO OF FRAMES ▽

Wadding
Light cardboard
40cm fabric
2.5cm lace
2m ribbon
Craft glue
Metal ring

Cut two backs 13cm x 9.5cm and one front 11.5cm x 8cm for each frame, from cardboard. Cut a back and front from paper first to check photograph position. Make cutting for oval shape. (Our oval shape was 8cm x 5cm).

Cover one of back pieces with fabric and the other with wadding and fabric. Glue to secure.

Join uncovered sides together with fabric covered piece at back. Glue lace to edge of padded back section before joining two pieces.

Cover front with oval shape, with wadding and fabric, snipping curves to make the fabric sit flat. Glue lace or braid around oval to decorate, if desired.

Glue three edges of front section to padded back section, leaving a long edge open to insert photograph.

Double ribbon and thread through ring for hanger. Place finished frames in desired positions on ribbon. Glue in place, and glue ribbon together.

CROCHETED LACE COAT HANGER COVER ▷

Note: Before commencing it is essential to first check your tension (see below)

YARN REQUIREMENTS:

4 Ply Cotton	1 ball (makes 3 covers)

Abbreviations: See page 125.
Accessories: One each 2.50mm and 1.25mm crochet hooks or SIZE REQUIRED TO GIVE CORRECT TENSION. 1 adult size coat hanger. 2.4m x 2cm-wide nylon lace, cut into 4 equal lengths. Sew a fine hem at each cut end of lace. 14cm of 2cm-wide satin ribbon, joined by sewing to cover hook. 50cm of 6mm-wide satin ribbon; scrap of polyester wadding; lining fabric 42cm x 13cm, sewn to cover coat hanger, leaving one end open.
Tension: 22 treble to 10cm.
Note: The chain at the beginning of each row will be counted as the first stitch.
Using a 2.50mm crochet hook make 89ch.
1st Row: 1htr in 3rd ch from the hook, 1htr in each ch to the end. 88tr.
2nd Row: (right side) Attach lace as follows, change to a 1.25mm crochet hook, fold one length of lace in half, pin centre of lace to the 44th st, starting at the beginning of each row, work lace in evenly to suit each half as follows, insert hook into lace and first st, make 1dc, * insert hook into lace and next st, make 1dc, rep from * to end evenly easing the lace as you work.
88sts.
3rd Row: Change to a 2.50mm crochet hook, 3ch, 1tr in the next and each st to the end.
88sts.
Rep 2nd and 3rd rows 3 times.
10th Row: 3ch, 1tr in each of the next 42tr, 2ch, miss 2tr, 1tr in each of the next 43tr.
11th Row: 3ch, 1tr in each of the next 42tr, 2tr in the 2ch space, 1tr in each of the next 43tr.
88sts.
12th Row: 3ch, * miss 1st, 1tr into the next st, 1tr into the missed st, rep from * ending with 1tr in top of the turning ch.
13th Row: 1dc in each st to the end.
88sts.
Rep 12th and 13th rows once, then the 12th row once.
17th Row: 2ch, 1htr in each st to the end. Fasten off.
Remove hook from hanger. Pad the coat hanger with polyester wadding, by wrapping it around the hanger till firm and even, and measuring 2cm in depth. Cover hook with ribbon. Fit the lining over the hanger with the sewn edge to the top, sew up the open end. Measure halfway across the top, put the hook into place by easing it through the seam of the lining, and then into the coat hanger. Place crochet work over hanger, the hook will fit through the 2ch space, made on the 10th row, join crochet work together, by working 1 row of dc evenly around the edges, leaving the lace free, turn, * 3ch, 1dc in next dc, rep from * to the end. Fasten off. Tie a bow with the 6mm ribbon at the base of hook.

Frames by Neryl Hogan

Coat hanger covers by Margaret Metcalfe; framed potpourri by Neryl Hogan

◁ FRAMED POTPOURRI

Embroidery hoop/frame
Lace fabric
Lace edging
Ribbon
Craft glue
Dried flowers

Cut two pieces of lace fabric slightly larger than frame. Glue together leaving an opening and insert potpourri. Glue opening closed. Insert this potpourri bag into frame. Cut off excess lace around edges.

Glue lace edging around the frame from the back. Tie ribbon bows and glue in place with dried flowers to decorate.

VINE HEART POTPOURRI ▷

Thin green grapevine branches or purchased wreath
Coat hanger wire
1m ribbon
Small amount fabric
Dried flowers
Potpourri
Craft glue

Cut grapevine when green and wrap around two 30cm pieces of coat hanger wire. Secure bunches of vine together by wrapping single strands vine tightly around ends. Bend each wire piece into half a heart shape and secure together with single strands of vine.

Leave to dry for a few months. Dried wreath can be spray painted and decorated.

Cut three small rectangles fabric, approximately 10cm x 5cm. Fold in half with wrong sides together and stitch up side and across folded end. Hem the open end then turn out. Fill with potpourri and tie with ribbon.

Wind ribbon around vine heart and tie in a bow. Glue potpourri bags onto vine heart. Decorate with dried flowers.

Vine heart potpourri by Neryl Hogan

Tissue box by Neryl Hogan

TISSUE BOX HOUSE △

Heavy cardboard
Wadding (thin)
30cm main fabric
20cm contrasting fabric
Lace
Ribbon
Craft glue
Scraps of felt

Cut cardboard pieces from pattern at right. Cover all pieces except chimney with wadding.

Cover pieces A, B, D and E with main fabric and cover C pieces with contrasting fabric.

Tape chimney pieces together on the inside and reinforce by gluing a piece of felt on the inside.

Join sides A and ends B together with glue and hold in place with sticky tape.

Trim roof pieces C with lace. Place glue on bottom edges of chimney and gently press onto roof. Hold in place with tape until dry.

Place glue along top edges of house. Gently press roof onto house and hold in place with tape until dry.

Decorate front of house with doors and windows using felt, ribbon and lace. Glue in place where desired.

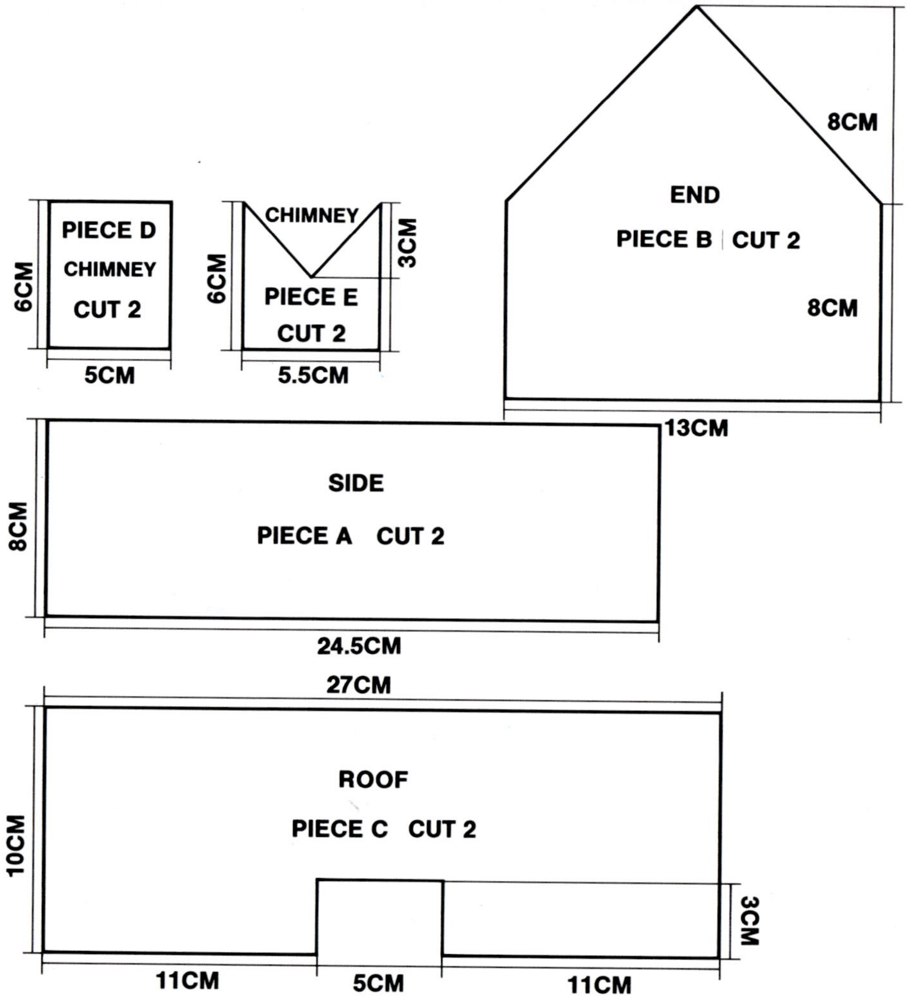

POTPOURRI PILLOW ▽

Two embroidered handkerchiefs
50cm polyester wadding
Scrap of fabric
Potpourri

Cut two large pieces of wadding 1cm smaller around all edges than handkerchief. Cut two small pieces of wadding about 5cm smaller around all edges than handkerchief.

Cut two squares of fabric approximately 10cm x 10cm. With right sides together stitch around three edges and turn out.

Insert potpourri inside fabric bag through open edge then handstitch edge closed. Place a small square of wadding either side of potpourri sachet then place a larger square of wadding on either side of the small squares.

Press all the creases out of handkerchiefs with an iron and place handkerchiefs on either side of the large wadding pieces. Pin edges together and baste.

Carefully machine stitch around edges to finish.

(Other cushion instructions overpage)

Potpourri: You can fill the pillow with a variety of fragrant herbs. Either buy them from a specialty shop or make your own combination. Here are some simple mixes. The ingredients are available from health food shops or chemists.

Lavender pouch: Mix together 1 cup of lavender flowers, 1 teaspoon orris root powder and 2 drops of lavender oil.

Eucalypt pillow: Select the dried eucalypt leaves of your choice and lightly crumble. Blend with a few drops of eucalyptus oil.

◁FRILLED CUSHION COVER WITH LACE

60cm fabric
1m double edged lace

Cut one piece fabric 36cm square. Stitch lace on as desired. We stitched two lengths parallel and cut out lace motifs and stitched them in the centre of lace rows.

Cut two pieces fabric 36 x 18cm and turn under one 36cm raw edge on each piece then turn under a 3cm hem and stitch.

Cut 2.2m of 8cm wide fabric and join into a continuous strip. Narrow hem one long edge and run gathering threads along the other edge. Pull up this frill to about 1.5m and pin raw edge around edge of the cushion front. Even gathers and join narrow ends of frill.

Overlap the hemmed edges of the cushion back pieces 6cm and pin onto cushion front piece with right sides together. Stitch around cushion, then finish raw edges.

Turn through to right side and press.

◁DOILEY COVERED CUSHION

50cm calico
1 large doiley

Cut one piece calico 48cm square. Stitch doiley in the centre of this piece (front).

Cut two pieces of calico 48 x 30cm. Turn back the raw edge along one 48cm length of each piece, then turn back and stitch a 3cm hem. Overlap both these pieces 6cm placing hems together to make cushion back.

Pin the cushion front (with doiley) right sides together with cushion back. Stitch around the edges using a 1cm seam and finish raw edges.

Turn cushion through opening to right side and press.

NAME PLAQUE▽

Heavy cardboard
Wadding
30cm fabric
Small amount contrast fabric
50cm ribbon
2m lace
Craft glue

Draw outlines of letters on cardboard, cut two of each letter. Draw backing shape as desired on cardboard and cut two backing shapes. Glue wadding to one of each letter and trim. Trace letters onto fabric and cut around allowing 1.5cm allowance. Fold allowance around to back of letter and glue in place. Curves need to be clipped. Cover each of the padded letters with fabric.

Glue lace to the back of each padded letter around edges. Cover remaining unpadded letters with fabric only. Glue unpadded letters to the back of the padded letters, wrong sides facing, to form a backing.

Construct backing in same manner as letters, padding front piece only. Attach ribbon to back of plaque for hanging. Glue letters in place on plaque.

Basket Liners by Susan Massey

Name plaque by Neryl Hogan

Potpourri by Neryl Hogan

◁ BASKET LINERS

Fabric (amount varies with basket size)
Lace
Ribbon
Polyester wadding
Craft glue

For basket with quilted base, cut two circles of fabric same size as base of the basket plus seam allowance. Cut one circle of polyester wadding.

For sides cut a strip of fabric as wide as the height of the basket wall and as long as the circumference of the basket, plus allowance for the turning.

To make the base put the piece of wadding between the two circles of fabric, pin around edge to hold in place. Make rows of stitching 2cm apart across the circle in one direction, then do the same in the other direction to quilt base.

For sides, join the narrow ends of the fabric strip together, then hem one side and gather the other. Pull in gathers to fit base and stitch sides to base.

Stitch lace to hemmed edge and decorate with ribbon and bows. Liner can be attached to basket by gluing or stitching.

Note: For basket with plain base cut one circle fabric and omit quilting.

BABY DOLL POTPOURRI ▽

1 face bead or plain bead painted with features
20cm x 11cm lace
30cm narrow ribbon
Fabric flowers
Potpourri
Craft glue

Thread 16cm of ribbon through hole in bead and double to form loop for hanging.

Fold lace in half, wrong sides together and glue along sides. Leave until dry.

Turn to right side. Fill with potpourri and tie ribbon around bag neck.

Glue bottom of face into gathered top of bag. Decorate with flowers.

For THE BATHROOM

Here's a steaming hot selection of bathroom ideas; all pretty and useful! Show off your creative flair with quick crochet trims on towels and washers. Line a basket – it looks great and is practical too; embroider a geometric border to make towels smart or knit up a tissue box cover. Turn the pages for more ideas with which to stack your stall.

RIGHT: Hand Towel and Washer with Cross Stitch Trim; Crocheted Heart Towel Edging; Rectangular Tissue Box Cover.

Tissue box cover by Margaret Metcalfe; cross stitch trim by Robyn Birkenshaw

◁ CROCHETED HEART TOWEL EDGING

Note: Before commencing it is essential to first check your tension (see below)

MEASUREMENTS		
Width (approx)	CM	8

YARN REQUIREMENTS:	
Patons Gem 4 Ply (50g) Balls	1 ball will make approx 120cm of edging

Abbreviations: See page 125. Additional abbreviations below.
Accessories: 2mm (No. 14) crochet hook or SIZE NEEDED TO GIVE CORRECT TENSION.
Additional Abbreviations: "Picot" = 3ch, sl st back into first of these ch; "A St" = * (yoh) twice, draw up a loop in next dc, (yoh and draw through first 2 loops on hook) twice*, miss 2dc, rep from * to *, yoh and draw through all 3 loops on hook.
Tension: 28 tr and 13.5 rows to 10cm over treble fabric, using 2mm hook. To achieve the desired effect, this item has been designed to be worked on a smaller hook at a tighter tension than usually recommended.

HEART

Make 17ch.
1st Row: Miss 7ch, 1tr in next ch, (2ch, miss 2ch, 1tr in next ch) 3 times.
2nd, 3rd and 4th Rows: (1dc, 1ch) in first tr, (2ch, miss 2ch, 1tr in next tr) 3 times, 2ch, 1tr in 3rd ch of turning ch.
5th Row: Work around 2 sides of square thus — 1ch, 3dc in each of next 2 sps, 5ch, 3dc in next sp, 7dc in next sp (corner sp), 3dc in next sp, 5ch, 3dc in each of next 2 sps, turn.
6th Row: 1ch, (1dtr, 1ch) 10 times and 1dtr all in next 5ch loop, 1dc in centre dc of 7dc (corner), (1dtr, 1ch) 10 times and 1dtr all in next 5ch loop, sl st in last dc. DO NOT TURN.
7th Row: 1ch, 3dc in each of next 3 sps down side of square, 7dc in corner sp, 3dc in each of next 3 sps up side of square, 1dc in next dtr, (1dc in ch sp, 1dc in dtr) 10 times (place a marker in 7th of these 20dc — we suggest a safety pin), 1dc in next dtr, (1dc in ch sp, 1dc in dtr) 10 times (place a marker in 13th of these 20dc), sl st in first dc.
Fasten off.
Make the number of hearts required (we used 5 for each end of hand towel and 9 for each end of bath towel) and join as follows:
1st Row: With right side facing, join yarn with a sl st where first marker was placed, (1dc, 2ch) in same place as sl st, * 2ch, miss 2dc, 1tr in next dc, 2ch, miss 2dc, 1dc in next dc, 2ch, miss 2dc, 1tr in next dc, 2ch, miss 2dc, "A St", rep from * once, working first "leg" of "A St" in second marked st and second "leg" in first marked st on next heart **, rep from * to **, ending last rep with 1dtr in last marked st instead of "A St".
2nd Row: (1dc, 1ch) in first dtr, * 2ch, miss 2ch, 1tr in next st, rep from * to end, working last tr in 3rd ch of turning ch loop.
3rd Round: 1ch, 3dc in each sp to last sp, 4dc in last sp, 1ch, "Picot", 1ch, 1dc in top of dtr, 1ch, "Picot", 1ch, 1dc in side of dtr, 1ch, "Picot", 1ch, 1dc in 2nd free dc along side of heart, * 1ch, "Picot", 1ch, miss 2dc, 1dc in next dc *, ** rep from * to * 10 times, 1dc in corresponding dc on next heart, rep from ** omitting 1dc at end of last rep, rep from * to * once, 1ch, "Picot", 1ch, 1dc in side of next row, 1ch, "Picot", 1ch, 1dc in base of next row, 1ch, "Picot", 1ch, 1dc in 1ch at beg.
Fasten off.

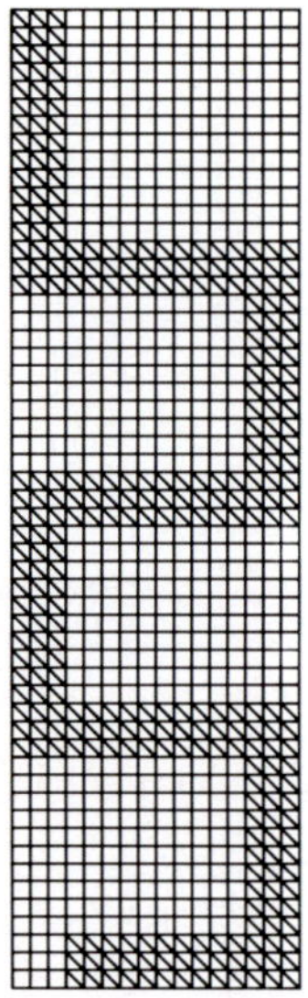

◁ HAND TOWEL AND WASHER WITH CROSS STITCH TRIM

Hand towel and washer
Cross stitch fabric strip
Stranded embroidery thread

Work design above using two strands of thread in colour of your choice on strip of fabric, allowing edge for turning under.

Press under raw edges along each strip of worked design and pin in place on washer and hand towel. Tack in place then machine stitch.

◁ RECTANGULAR TISSUE BOX COVER

Note: Before commencing it is essential to first check your tension (see below)

MEASUREMENTS
Completed cover has 72cm circumference

YARN REQUIREMENTS:	
4 Ply Cotton (50g) Ball	1

Abbreviations: See page 125.
Accessories: 2.50mm and 1.25mm crochet hooks, or SIZE REQUIRED TO GIVE CORRECT TENSION.
7 metres of 2cm-wide nylon lace, cut into 7 x 1 metre lengths, sew ends together to make 7 circles; 50cm of 6mm-wide ribbon; tissue box, sized to hold 150 tissues; small quantity of hat elastic to thread through the 1st row to keep the cover firm over box.
Tension: 22tr to 10cm.
Note: There should be 158sts after the completion of each row till the shaping.
Starting at the base, using a 2.50mm crochet hook make 158ch, join with a sl st to form a ring, making sure not to twist work when joining.
1st Round: 3ch, 1tr in each ch to the end, join with a sl st in the top of the 3ch made at the beg.
2nd, 3rd and 4th Rounds: 3ch, 1tr in each tr to the end, join with a sl st in top of 3ch made at the beg.
5th Round: Change to a 1.25mm crochet hook. Take a prepared lace circle and pin it to work at quarter points. Attach lace as follows, insert hook into lace and same place as sl st make 1dc, * insert hook into lace and next st make 1dc, evenly easing the lace as you work, rep from * to end join with a sl st in 1st dc made.
6th Round: Change to a 2.50mm hook. 3ch, 1tr in each st to the end, join with a sl st in top of 3ch made at beg.

158 tr.
Rep 5th and 6th rounds 6 times.

SHAPE TOP

3ch, 1tr in each of the next 22tr, miss 4tr, 1tr in each of the next 48tr, miss 4tr, 1tr in each of the next 23tr, miss 4tr, 1tr in each of the next 48tr, miss 4tr, join with a sl st in top of the 3ch made at the beg.

2nd Round: Sl st over the next 2tr, 3ch, 1tr in each of the next 18tr, miss 4tr, 1tr in each of the next 44tr, miss 4tr, 1tr in each of the next 19tr, miss 4tr, 1tr in each of the next 44tr, join with a sl st in top of 3ch made at the beg.

3rd Round: Sl st over the next 2tr, 3ch, 1tr in each of the next 14tr, miss 4tr, 1tr in each of the next 40tr, miss 4tr, 1tr in each of the next 15tr, miss 4tr, 1tr in each of the next 40tr, join with a sl st in top of 3ch made at the beg.

4th Round: Sl st over the next 2tr, 3ch, 1tr in each of the next 10tr, miss 4tr, 1tr in each of the next 36tr, miss 4tr, 1tr in each of the next 11tr, miss 4tr, 1tr in each of the next 36tr, join with a sl st in the top of the 3ch made at the beg.

5th Round: Sl st over the next 2tr, 3ch, 1tr in each of the next 6tr, miss 4tr, 1tr in each of the next 32tr, miss 4tr, 1tr in each of the next 7tr, miss 4tr, 1tr in each of the next 32tr, join with a sl st in top of 3ch made at the beg.

6th Round: Sl st over the next 2tr, 3ch, 1tr in each of the next 2tr, miss 4tr, 1tr in each of the next 28tr, miss 4tr, 1tr in each of the next 3tr, miss 4tr, 1tr in each of the next 28tr, join with a sl st in the top of the 3ch made at the beg.

7th Round: Sl st over the next tr, 3ch, miss 3tr, 1tr in each of the next 24tr, miss 3tr, 1tr in the next tr, miss 3tr, 1tr in each of the next 24tr, join with a sl st in the top of the 3ch made at the beg.

8th Round: Work 1 round of crab stitch as follows, insert hook from front into the last st made, yoh, draw through work only (2 loops on hook), yoh and draw through both loops on the hook, * working *back* along the last row made, insert the hook into the next st, yoh and draw through work only (2 loops on hook), yoh and draw through both loops on hook, rep from* to end, join with a sl st in first st made. Fasten off.

Cut ribbon in half, make 2 bows, sew 1 bow at each end of the opening. If needed thread a length of hat elastic through the first row, this will keep the cover firm over the tissue box.

TOILET ROLL HOLDER ▽

Heavy cardboard
1m cotton fabric
2m lace
2m braid
Wadding
Dried flowers

Cut two large cardboard back pieces, 87cm x 44cm (taper top corners if desired). Cut one piece cardboard, 80cm x 31cm (for roll).

Glue wadding to one back piece and cover with fabric. Cover other back piece with fabric. Glue lace to wrong side of back piece around the edge.

To make hanger for back piece, pierce holes in fabric covered back piece and glue or tape braid loop in place on wrong side.

Glue two back pieces together with wrong sides facing. Trim with braid, if desired.

Cover roll piece with fabric and glue lace to wrong side around edge. Trim with braid around edges.

Glue this piece in place so top edge is one-quarter way down back section and bottom rolls under as pictured below.

LINED BASKET ▷

Fabric (amount varies with basket size)
Wadding
Lace
Ribbon
Craft glue
Spray adhesive
Basket
Cardboard

Cut a cardboard piece to fit basket base. Glue wadding onto cardboard using spray adhesive, trim wadding to fit cardboard. Cut a piece of fabric to fit cardboard, plus 1.5cm allowance. Cover padded cardboard with fabric gluing the allowance to cardboard back.

Measure the circumference of the basket and add half this amount again to give length of wall piece. Measure basket wall width from inside base to height desired and add 1.5cm allowance to give width of wall piece. Cut two pieces of fabric to give the wall section.

Join wall sections with side seams. Run a gathering thread around the base edge. Hem the top edge of the wall piece. If using lace or contrast fabric frill, stitch around the top edge of the wall piece. Make ▷

Toilet roll holder by Neryl Hogan

a casing for ribbon or run gathering threads around the top edge of the wall piece. Place wall piece into basket and pull up gathering to fit.

If using a casing insert ribbons and leave a gap in the wall side seams unstitched for the ribbon ties. Glue wall section into basket. Glue base into basket over wall section at base.

Decorate with ribbon bows.

◣ RED ● WHITE
☒ GREY ◹ TAN

Basket by Elsie May

BATHROOM SET WITH GEESE MOTIF ▷

Note: Before commencing it is essential to first check your tension (see below)

MEASUREMENTS		
Tissue Box Cover		
Length (approx)	CM	22
	INS	8.75
Height (approx)	CM	8
	INS	3.25
Toilet Roll Cover		
Height (approx)	CM	10.5
	INS	4.25

YARN REQUIREMENTS:	
Patons Gem 4 Ply (50g) Balls	
Tissue Box Cover	1
Toilet Roll Cover	1

Abbreviations: See page 125.
Accessories: 1 pair 2.75mm (No. 12) knitting needles or SIZE NEEDED TO GIVE CORRECT TENSION. Stranded embroidery thread (see key for colours); length of lace; tissue box (length — 23cm, width — 11.5cm and height — 8cm).
Tension: 29 sts and 38.5 rows to 10cm over stocking stitch.

TISSUE BOX COVER
Cast on 60 sts.
Knit 5 rows garter st (1st row is wrong side), inc 4 sts evenly across last row.
64 sts.
Next Row: Knit.
Next Row: K2, purl to last 2 sts, K2.
Rep last 2 rows 14 times.
Work 14 rows stocking st, omitting garter st borders.
Next Row: Knit.
Next Row: P14, K36, P14.
Rep last 2 rows once.
Divide for opening: 1st Row: K17, cast off 30 sts, K17.
Cont on last 17 sts.
Next Row: P14, K3.
Next Row: Knit.
Next Row: P14, K3.
Break off yarn.
Join yarn to rem 17 sts and work 3 rows stocking st, beg with a purl row and having 3 garter sts at opening edge.
Next Row: K17, cast on 30 sts, knit across rem 17 sts.
64 sts.
Next Row: P14, K36, P14.
Next Row: Knit.
Next Row: P14, K36, P14.
Work a further 14 rows stocking st.
Next Row: Knit.
Next Row: K2, purl to last 2 sts, K2.
Rep last 2 rows 14 times, dec 4 sts evenly across last row.
60 sts.
Knit 5 rows garter st.
Cast off.

SIDE PANELS
With right side facing, knit up 31 sts evenly along side edge between garter st borders.
1st Row: K2, purl to last 2 sts, K2.
2nd Row: Knit.
Rep 1st and 2nd rows 14 times, then 1st row once, dec 2 sts evenly across last row.
29 sts.
Knit 5 rows garter st.
Cast off.

TO MAKE UP:
Use six strands of thread and refer to key for colours. Using knitting stitch (see page 126), embroider geese from graph above. Embroider eyes in straight stitch. Outline white goose in stem stitch using grey thread. With a slightly damp cloth and warm iron, press lightly. Using a flat seam, join corners. Sew lace around top edge as pictured.

TOILET ROLL COVER
TOP
Cast on 11 sts.
1st Row: Knit.
Working in stocking st (beg with a purl row), cast on 2 sts at beg of next 10 rows.
31 sts.
Inc at each end of alt rows 3 times.
37 sts.
Work a further 15 rows stocking st, beg with a purl row.
Dec at each end of next and alt rows 3 times in all.
31 sts.
Work 1 row.
Cast off 2 sts at beg of next 10 rows.
11 sts.
Cast off.
BASE
Cast on 100 sts.
Knit 5 rows garter st (1st row is wrong side), inc 8 sts evenly across last row.
108 sts.
Work in stocking st until work measures 10.5cm from beg, ending with a purl row.
Cast off.
TO MAKE UP:
Using knitting stitch, embroider geese from graph as for Tissue Box Cover. With a slightly damp cloth and warm iron, press lightly. Using back stitch, join base seam then sew base to top, inserting lace as you go.

SOAP COVER▷

YARN REQUIREMENTS:	
4 ply Cotton (50g) Ball	1 ball makes approximately 6 covers

Abbreviations: See page 125.
Accessories: 2.50mm and 1.25mm crochet hooks or SIZE REQUIRED TO GIVE CORRECT TENSION.
1.2 metres of 1cm wide lace cut into 3 equal lengths, sew ends together to form 3 circles; 30cm of 6mm-wide ribbon; 1 cake of oval-shaped soap approximately 9cm in length.
COVER
Using a 2.50mm crochet hook, make 8ch, join with a sl st to form a ring.
1st Round: 3ch, work 17tr into the ring, join with a sl st in top of 3ch made at beginning.
18tr.
2nd Round: 3ch, 1tr in same place as sl st, 2tr in each tr to end, join with a sl st in top of 3ch made at beginning.
36tr.
3rd Round: 3ch, 1tr in same place as sl st, 2tr in each of the next 5tr, 1tr in each of the next 12tr, 2tr in each of the next 6tr, 1tr in each of the next 12tr, join with a sl st in top of 3ch made at beginning.
48tr.
4th Round: 3ch, 1tr in same place as sl st, (1tr in next tr, 2tr in next st) 5 times, 1tr in each of the next 13tr, (2tr in next tr, 1tr in next tr) 6 times, 1tr in each of the next 12tr, join with a sl st in top of 3ch made at beginning.
60tr.
5th Round: Change to a 1.25mm crochet hook. With right side facing and a prepared lace circle, insert hook into lace and same place as sl st make 1dc, * insert hook into lace and next st make 1dc, evenly easing the lace as you work, rep from * to end join with a sl st in 1st dc made.
6th Round: Change to a 2.50mm crochet hook, 3ch, 1tr in each st to the end join with a sl st into top of 3ch made at beginning, still having 60tr.
Rep rounds 5 and 6 once then the 5th round once.
11th Round: 4ch, * miss 1tr, 1tr into the next tr, 1ch, rep from * to the end, join with a sl st in the 3rd of the 4ch made at the beg.
Fasten off.
Thread ribbon through the 1ch spaces made in the last row, place soap in cover, tie ribbon in a bow.

Soap cover pictured overpage.

Soap cover by Margaret Metcalfe

to hold 45 tissues.
Tension: 22tr to 10cm.
Using a 2.50mm crochet hook make 104ch, join with a sl st in first ch made, making sure not to twist the work when joining.
1st Round: 3ch, 1tr in each ch to the end, join with a sl st in top of the 3ch made at the beg.
104tr.
2nd Round: 3ch, 1tr in each tr to the end, join with a sl st in top of 3ch made at beg.
3rd Round: same as the 2nd.
4th Round: Change to a 1.25mm crochet hook. Take a prepared lace circle and pin it to work at quarter points. Attach lace as follows, insert hook into lace and same place as sl st make 1dc, * insert hook into lace and next st make 1dc, evenly easing the lace as you work, rep from * to the end, join with a sl st in first dc made.
5th Round: Change to a 2.50mm crochet hook.
3ch, 1tr in each st to the end, join with a sl st in top of the 3ch made at

CROCHETED FACE WASHER EDGING ▷

YARN REQUIREMENTS:
4 Ply Cotton (50g) Ball — 1 ball makes 6 edgings

Abbreviations: See page 125.
Accessories: 1.75mm and 2.50mm crochet hooks; 1 face washer 30cm square.
Note: This is a 9 stitch pattern, if more dc are needed than stated add in multiples of 9dc to each side. If less dc are needed reduce by multiples of 9dc each side.
EDGING
Using a 1.75mm crochet hook, with right side of washer facing, starting in the centre of any corner, make 63dc evenly along the side of the washer to the centre of the next corner, * place a length of yarn in the 63rd dc (this will save counting from the beginning all the time), then work 63dc evenly from this corner to the centre of the next corner, rep from * till all sides have been worked, join with a sl st in the first dc made.
There will be 252dc altogether.
Change to a 2.50mm crochet hook.
Next Round: 4ch, 2dtr in the same place as the sl st, 1tr in each of the next 2dc, 1htr in the next dc, 1dc in the next dc, * 1dc in the next dc, 1htr in the next dc, 1tr in each of the next 2dc, 3dtr in the next dc, 1tr in each of the next 2dc, 1htr in the next dc, 1dc in the next dc, rep from * to the last 4dc, 1dc in the next dc, 1htr in the next dc, 1tr in each of the next 2dc, join with a sl st in top of 4ch made at the beg.
Fasten off, sew ends of yarn securely into washer.

CROCHETED SQUARE TISSUE BOX COVER ▷

MEASUREMENTS
Fits a square tissue box with 12cm sides

YARN REQUIREMENTS:
4 Ply Cotton (50g) Ball — 1 ball makes 2 covers

Abbreviations: See page 125.
Accessories: 2.50mm and 1.25mm crochet hooks or SIZE REQUIRED TO GIVE CORRECT TENSION. 3.5 metres of 1cm-wide nylon lace, cut into 5 equal lengths, sew ends together to make 5 circles; 40cm of 6mm-wide ribbon; 1 tissue box sized

Edgings and tissue box cover by Margaret Metcalfe

the beg.
104sts.
Rep 4th and 5th rounds 3 times, then the 4th round once.

SHAPE TOP

Change to a 2.50mm crochet hook. 3ch, 1tr in each of the next 21sts, miss 4sts, * 1tr in each of the next 22sts, miss 4sts, rep from * twice, join with a sl st in top of 3ch made at beg.

Next Round: Sl st over the next 2sts, 3ch, 1tr in each of the next 3tr, 1htr in each of the next 3tr, 1dc in each of the next 4sts, 1htr in each of the next 3sts, 1tr in each of the next 4sts, miss 4tr, * 1tr in each of the next 4tr, 1htr in each of the next 3tr, 1dc in each of the next 4sts, 1htr in each of the next 3sts, 1tr in each of the next 4sts, miss 4sts, rep from * twice, join with a sl st in the top of 3ch made at the beg.

Next Round: Sl st over the next 2tr, 3ch, 1tr in each of the next 2sts, 1htr in each of the next 3sts, 1dc in each of the next 2sts, 1htr in each of the next 3sts, 1tr in each of the next 3sts, miss 4sts, * 1tr in each of the next 3sts, 1htr in each of the next 3sts, 1dc in each of the next 2sts, 1htr in each of the next 3sts, 1tr in each of the next 3sts, miss 4sts, rep from * twice, join with a sl st in top of the 3ch made at the beg.

Work one round of crab stitch as follows, insert hook **back** into the last st made, yoh, draw through work only (2 loops on hook), yoh and draw through both loops on hook * working **back along** the row insert hook into the next st, yoh, and draw through (2 loops on hook), yoh and draw through both loops, rep from * to end join with a sl st in first st made. Fasten off.

Make 2 bows out of the ribbon, sew opposite each other on the last row worked. If needed, thread a length of elastic through the first row, this will keep cover firm over box.

▽ ROSE TRIM & EDGING FOR FACE WASHER

YARN REQUIREMENTS:	
4 Ply Cotton (50g) Ball	1 ball makes up to 6 trims

Abbreviations: See page 125.
Accessories: 1.75mm and 2.50mm crochet hooks; small cake of rose shaped soap; 1 face washer.

EDGING

Using a 1.75mm crochet hook and 4 ply cotton * insert hook about 1cm in from face washer edge, work (2dc, 4ch sl st in first of the 4ch, 2dc) all in the same place, miss about 1cm, rep from * to the end, join with a sl st in the first dc made.
Fasten off.

ROSE TRIM

Use a 2.50mm crochet hook, make 6ch, join with a sl st to form a ring.

1st Round: 6ch, * 1tr into ring, 3ch, work from * 5 times, sl st in 3rd of 6ch made at the beg (there will be six 3ch spaces).

2nd Round: (1dc, 1htr, 3tr, 1htr, 1dc) in each 3ch space to the end, join with a sl st in first dc made. There will be 6 petals.

3rd Round: Fold petal forward as you work, * 5ch, working into back of work 1dc around the tr of the first round between petals, rep from * omitting dc on last rep, join with a sl st around the tr of the first round and the first 5ch loop of this round. There will be 6 loops.

4th Round: (1dc, 1htr, 5tr, 1htr, 1dc) in each 5ch loop to the end, join with a sl st in the first dc made.

5th Round: Fold petal forward as you work, * 7ch, working into back of work 1dc around the next dc of the 3rd round between the petals, rep from * omitting dc at the end of last rep join with a sl st around the dc of the round between the petals and the first 7ch loop of this round.

6th Round: (1dc, 1htr, 4tr, 3ch sl st into top of last tr made, 3tr, 1htr, 1dc) in each 7ch loop to the end, join with a sl st in first dc made.
Fasten off.

Sew rose to face washer, leaving two petals free towards the centre to put in a rose shaped cake of soap.

For CHILDREN

If you can't bear to throw away left over fabric and yarn, here are some great ways to use it! A small amount of yarn will make hand puppets, teddy toys and baby's blocks; use felt scraps for children's jewellery and transform fabric remnants into friendly animal pencil cases. A fete wouldn't be complete without baby wear, so we've included adorable knitted and crocheted designs as well as clever ways to pretty-up plain whites by adding embroidery and lace.

RIGHT: Grub Rose Nappy, Singlet, Socks and Bib (instructions overpage).

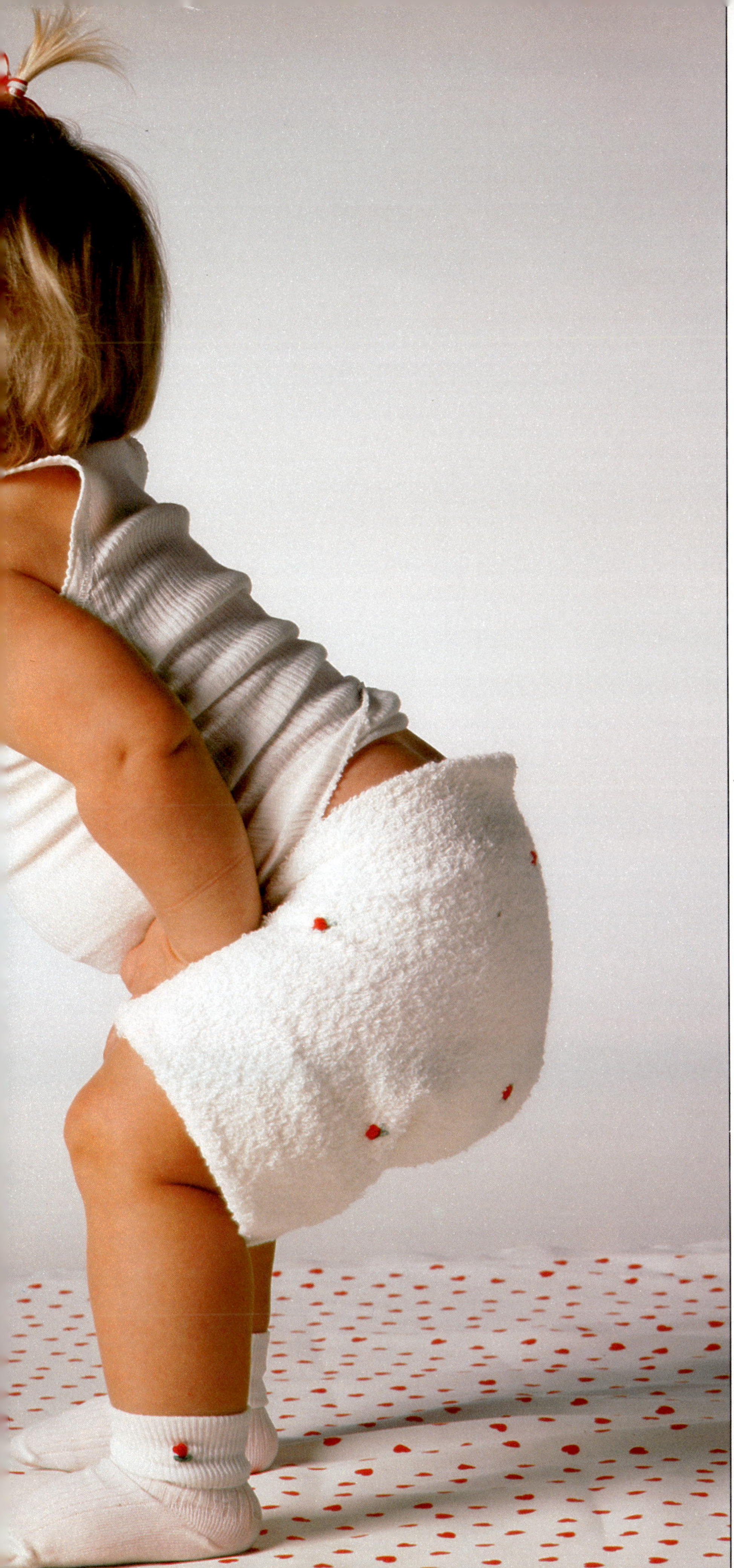

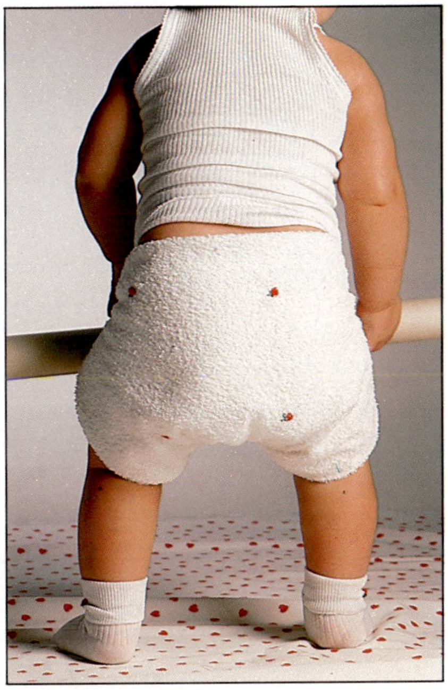

Fabric from Coloroll

GRUB ROSE NAPPY, SINGLET, SOCKS AND BIB

Nappy
Baby singlet
Baby socks
Bib
50cm broderie anglaise edging
Stranded embroidery thread

Embroider nappy, singlet, socks and bib with bullion stitch using two strands of thread. Embroider leaves using stem stitch and two strands of thread. See page 126 for stitch instructions. Use colours of your choice.

Pin broderie anglaise edging around bib and machine stitch.

FRUIT SALAD HAIR COMBS

2 hair combs
Scraps of felt in yellow, green, red, blue, purple
Cardboard
Craft glue

Draw fruit shapes onto cardboard and cut out. Glue cardboard shapes to felt (eg bananas, yellow felt; strawberries, red felt), and cut out felt. For pineapple glue green to top and yellow to bottom. Draw on fruit detail with a black pen.

Before gluing shapes to comb, rough the comb surface with a nail file for better grip. Position and glue fruit. Allow sufficient drying time before wearing.

FELT BRACELET

Two 18cm x 5cm strips of bright felt fabric
Four contrasting buttons
15cm elastic

Position and stitch buttons onto one piece of felt. Make sure the buttons are stitched on securely. Take a second strip of felt for the underside and sew long seams together with buttons facing out.

Thread elastic through casing and stitch ends of elastic together so felt bangle gathers up slightly. Stitch ends of felt together to cover elastic.

BUNNY TISSUE AND TALC COVERS

Note: Before commencing it is essential to first check your tension (see below)

MEASUREMENTS

Tissue Box Cover		
Length (approx)	CM	22
	INS	8.75
Height (approx)	CM	8
	INS	3.25
Talc Cover		Fits a 250g tin of talc

YARN REQUIREMENTS

Patons Patonyle 4 Ply or **Fairytale 4 Ply** (50g) Balls	
Tissue Box Cover	1
Talc Cover	1
Or Patons 4 Ply Feathersoft (25g) Balls	
Tissue Box Cover	2
Talc Cover	1

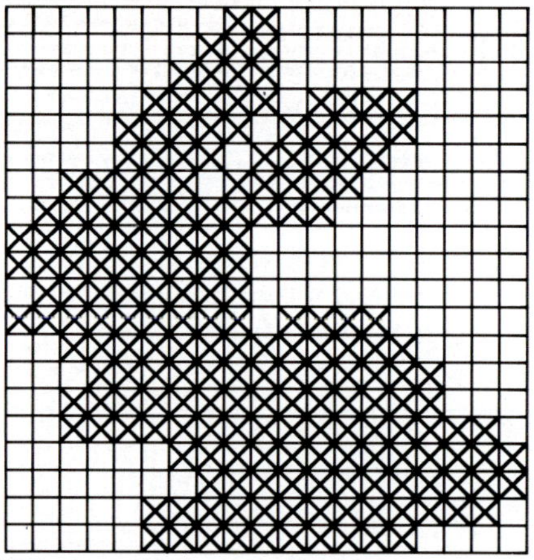

☒ **KNITTING STITCH**

Accessories: 1 pair each 3.25mm (No. 10) knitting needles or SIZE NEEDED TO GIVE CORRECT TENSION. 3mm (No. 10-11) crochet hook; embroidery thread; ribbon for talc cover; tissue box (Length-23cm, Width-11.5cm and Height-8cm).

Abbreviations: "Picot" = 3ch, sl st in first of these ch.

Tension: 29 sts and 38.5 rows to 10cm over stocking stitch using 3.25mm needles.

TISSUE BOX COVER

Cast on 60 sts.

Knit 5 rows garter st (1st row is wrong side), inc 4 sts evenly across last row.

64 sts.

Next Row: Knit.

Next Row: K2, purl to last 2 sts, K2.

Jewellery by Jillian Morrow

Rep last 2 rows 14 times.
Work 14 rows stocking st, omitting garter st borders.
Next Row: Knit.
Next Row: P14, K36, P14.
Rep last 2 rows once.
Divide for opening: 1st Row: K17, cast off 30 sts, K17.
Cont on last 17 sts.
Next Row: P14, K3.
Next Row: Knit.
Next Row: P14, K3.
Break off yarn.
Join yarn to rem 17 sts and work 3 rows stocking st, beg with a purl row and having 3 garter sts at opening edge.
Next Row: K17, cast on 30 sts, knit across rem 17 sts.
64 sts.
Next Row: P14, K36, P14.
Next Row: Knit.
Next Row: P14, K36, P14.
Work a further 14 rows stocking st.
Next Row: Knit.
Next Row: K2, purl to last 2 sts, K2.
Rep last 2 rows 14 times, dec 4 sts evenly across last row.
60 sts.
Knit 5 rows garter st.
Cast off.

SIDE PANELS

With right side facing, knit up 31 sts evenly along side edge between garter st borders.
1st Row: K2, purl to last 2 sts, K2.
2nd Row: Knit.
Rep 1st and 2nd rows 14 times, then 1st row once, dec 2 sts evenly across last row.
29 sts.
Knit 5 rows garter st.
Cast off.

TO MAKE UP:

Using knitting stitch and six strands of thread, embroider rabbit from graph.
DO NOT PRESS FAIRYTALE OR FEATHERSOFT. With a slightly damp cloth press PATONYLE stocking stitch lightly. Using a flat seam, join corners.

TALC COVER

Cast on 12 sts.
1st Row: Inc in each st to last st, K1.
2nd and Alt Rows: Purl.
3rd Row: * K1, inc in next st, rep from * to last st, K1.
5th Row: * K2, inc in next st, rep from * to last st, K1.
7th Row: * K3, inc in next st, rep from * to last st, K1.
8th Row: Inc in first st, purl to end.
57 sts.
Work in stocking st until work measures 14.5cm (or length required) from beg, ending with a purl row.
Cast off loosely.

EDGING

Using hook, work 52dc evenly along cast-off edge.
1st Row: (1dc, 1ch) in first dc, * 2ch, miss 2dc, 1tr in next dc, rep from * to end.
2nd Row: 1ch, 1dc in first tr, * (1dc, "Picot", 1dc) in next 2ch sp, 1dc in next tr, rep from * working last dc in 3rd ch of turning ch.
3rd Row: 1ch, 1dc in first dc, * 5ch, miss 2dc, 1dc in next dc, rep from * to end.
4th Row: 1ch, * (2dc, "Picot", 2dc) in next 5ch loop, rep from * to end.
Fasten off.

TO MAKE UP:

Using knitting stitch, embroider rabbit from graph as illustrated. See page 126 for stitch instructions. Use six strands of thread in colour of your choice. DO NOT PRESS FAIRYTALE OR FEATHERSOFT. Press PATONYLE stocking stitch lightly. Using back stitch for stocking stitch and flat seam for crochet, join back seam. Thread ribbon through first row of edging. Place talc inside cover, draw up ribbon, tie bow at front.

HAND PUPPETS

Note: Before commencing it is essential to first check your tension (see below)		
YARN REQUIREMENTS		
Villawool Tasman 8 Ply (100g) Balls		
	Dog	**Cat**
White (W)	¼	¼
Blue (B)	¼	
Red (R)		⅓

Abbreviations: See page 125.
Accessories: 1 pair 4mm (No. 8) and 1 set 4mm (No. 8) knitting needles or SIZE NEEDED TO GIVE CORRECT TENSION; polyester fibre fill; cardboard tube 4cm in diameter and 2.5cm long for each puppet; small piece of cotton fabric; stranded embroidery thread for features; length of ribbon and 3 buttons for Cat.
Tension: 22.5 sts and 29.5 rows to 10cm over stocking stitch, using 4mm needles. If less sts use smaller needles, if more sts use bigger needles.

DOG PUPPET

HEAD: Right Side Section (beg at neck)
Using W, cast on 10 sts.
Work 3 rows stocking st, beg with a purl row.
Cast on 3 sts at beg of next row and foll alt row (front edge).
Inc at beg of next and alt rows 3 times in all (back edge).
19 sts.
Work 2 rows stocking st.
Cast off 4 sts at beg of next row (front edge), then dec at end of foll row.
Work 1 row.
Dec at each end of next 3 rows.
8 sts.
Cast off.

Left Side Section
Working knit for purl and purl for knit throughout, work as for Right Side Section.

Centre Section (beg at front neck edge)
Using W, cast on 4 sts.
Beg with a purl row, work 4 rows stocking st, inc at each end of 2nd and 4th rows.
8 sts.
Work 6 rows stocking st.
Dec at each end of next row and foll 3rd row.
4 sts.
Work 9 rows stocking st.
Inc at each end of next row and foll 6th row.
8 sts.
Work 29 rows stocking st. Cast off.

EARS
Using set of needles and W, cast on 16 sts.
5, 5, 6 sts.
Join into a round, taking care not to twist cast-on edge.
Knit 2 rounds.
3rd Round: Inc in first st, K7, place a marker (a loop of contrasting thread which will be slipped on each foll round) on needle, inc in next st, K7.
Cont inc in first st and in st after marker in foll 5th rounds 3 times.
24 sts.
Knit 4 rounds.
Dec at beg of round and after marker in next round and foll alt round.
20 sts.
Slip first 10 sts of round on to one needle and last 10 sts on to another needle and graft sts tog.

TO MAKE UP:
Do not press. Beg at front neck edge of each piece and using back stitch, join head sections tog as foll: First 10 rows of centre section to first 5 rows of side sections, next 8 rows to next 9 rows (straight edge for nose), next 5 rows to 4 cast-off sts, next 7 rows to last 6 rows of side sections; sew rem rows of centre section to cast-off edge of side sections and down back edge to back neck edge. Sew ears to head. Embroider face in straight and satin stitch (see page 126). Fill head firmly. Cover one end of cardboard tube with cotton fabric and place this end into head, keeping open end of tube at neck edge. Tack in place.

BODY

BACK
Using B, cast on 32 sts.
Knit 3 rows garter st (1st row is wrong side).
Working in stripes of 6 rows B and 2 rows W throughout, work 26 rows stocking st. Tie a coloured thread at each end of last row to mark beg of armholes.
Cont in stripes, dec at each end of next and foll 6th rows 4 times in all.
24 sts.
Work 1 row. Tie a coloured thread at each end of last row to mark end of armholes.
Shape shoulders: Dec at each end of next and alt rows 4 times in all.
16 sts.
Work 1 row. Cast off.

FRONT
Using B, cast on 28 sts.
Work as for Back, noting that there will be 20 sts at end of armhole shaping and 12 sts at end of

ılder shaping.
MS (beg at top)
ng B, cast on 30 sts.
king in stripes of 12 rows B and
ws W, work in stocking st, dec at
each end of 3rd and alt rows until 14 sts rem.
Work 1 row. Cast off.

TO COMPLETE

Using back stitch, join shoulder seams. Sew arms in position between coloured threads. Join side and arm seams. Sew neck edge to neck edge of head.

CAT PUPPET

HEAD (beg at neck edge)

Using set of needles and W, cast on 28 sts.
9, 9, 10 sts.
Join into a round, taking care not to twist cast-on edge.
Knit 2 rounds.
3rd Round: Inc in first st, K23, inc in next st, K3 (centre front).
4th, 6th, 8th and 10th Rounds: Knit.
5th Round: Inc in first st, K25, inc in next st, K3.
7th Round: Inc in first st, K10, inc in next st, K5 (centre back), inc in next st, K10, inc in next st, K3.
9th Round: Inc in first st, K31, inc in next st, K3.
11th Round: K14, inc in next st, K5, inc in next st, K17.
40 sts.
12th Round: K1, K2 tog, K32, K2 tog, K3.
13th, 15th, 17th and 19th Rounds: Knit.
14th Round: K2, K2 tog, K28, K2 tog, K4 .
16th Round: K3, K2 tog, K7, K2 tog, K6, K2 tog, K7, K2 tog, K5.
18th Round: K4, (K2 tog, K4, K2 tog, K6) twice.
20th Round: K5, K2 tog, K1, K2 tog, K6, K2 tog, K1, K2 tog, K7.
24 sts.
Knit first 5 sts of round. Slip next 12 sts on to one needle for back of head, slip rem 12 sts on to another needle for front of head and graft sts tog.

EARS

Using W, cast on 14 sts.
Work 2 rows stocking st.
Dec at each end of next and alt rows until 8 sts rem.
Work 1 row. Cast off (top edge).

TO MAKE UP:

Do not press. Using back stitch, join side edges of ears, forming a point at top edge. Fold ear so that seam is at centre of inner ear and sew to head as illustrated. Embroider features as pictured. Fill head firmly. Cover one end of cardboard tube with cotton fabric and place this end into head, keeping open end of tube at neck edge. Tack in place.

BODY

Work as for Dog Puppet, working in R throughout.

ARMS

Work as for Dog Puppet, using R in place of B.

TO COMPLETE

Work as for Dog Puppet. Sew on buttons as pictured. Tie ribbon around neck.

▽GRUB ROSE ALL-IN-ONE

Cotton all-in-one for baby
Stranded embroidery thread

Work bullion stitch roses around neck edge of all-in-one using two strands of thread in any colour.

Embroider leg edges using straight stitch worked in a zigzag pattern using two strands of thread.

See page 126 for stitch instructions.

TEDDY TOY AND CRIB STRING▽

Note: Before commencing it is essential to first check your tension (see below)

MEASUREMENTS

Height (approx)		
	CM	12
	INS	5

YARN REQUIREMENTS

Patons 3 Ply Feathersoft or **Baby Wool 3 Ply** (25g) Balls

Contrast 1 (C1)	small quantity
Contrast 2 (C2)	small quantity

Abbreviations: See page 125.
Accessories: One pr 2mm (No. 14) knitting needles or SIZE REQUIRED TO GIVE CORRECT TENSION; 1.75mm steel crochet hook; contrasting yarn or embroidery thread in colour of your choice; polyester fibre fill; 1m ribbon; 50cm hat elastic; 3 bells.
Tension: 21 sts and 27.5 rows to 5cm over stocking st.

HEAD

Using C1, cast on 11 sts.
Work 4 rows stocking st.
** **5th Row:** Inc in first st, knit to last 2 sts, inc in next st, K1.
6th Row: Purl.
Rep 5th and 6th rows 3 times.
19 sts.
Work 4 rows stocking st.
Dec at each end of next and alt rows until 11 sts rem. **
Work 1 row stocking st.
Rep from ** to ** once.
Work 5 rows stocking st.
Cast off.
Join side seams.

EARS (2)

Using C1, cast on 9 sts.
Work in stocking st, dec at each end of 3rd and alt rows until 3 sts rem.
Inc at each end of alt rows until there are 9 sts.
Work 1 row stocking st.
Cast off.
Fold in half with right side outside and oversew side edges.

MUZZLE

Using C1, cast on 21 sts.
Work 2 rows stocking st.
3rd Row: K2, sl 1, K2 tog, psso, (K4, sl 1, K2 tog, psso) twice, K2.
4th Row: Purl.
5th Row: K1, sl 1, K2 tog, psso, (K2, sl 1, K2 tog, psso) twice, K1.
9 sts.
Break off yarn, run end through rem sts, draw up and fasten securely, join seam.

BODY AND LEGS

Using C2, cast on 38 sts.
Work 16 rows stocking st, in stripes of 4 rows C2, 2 rows C1, 6 rows C2, 2 rows C1 and 2 rows C2.
Using C2, **17th Row:** K3, (K2 tog, K4) 5 times, K2 tog, K3.
18th Row: Purl.
19th Row: K1, (K2 tog, K2) 7 times, K2 tog, K1.
24 sts.
20th Row: Purl.
Cast off.
Join side seam.
With right side facing and using C2, knit up 8 sts on each side of seam at cast-on edge.
16 sts.
Work 19 rows stocking st (beg with a purl row) in stripes of 1 row C2, (2 rows C1 and 6 rows C2) twice, then 2 rows C1.
Cast off.
Missing 3 sts in centre of back and front; using C2, knit up 16 sts along cast-on edge and work other leg in same manner.
Join leg and crotch seams.

ARMS (2)

Using C2, cast on 15 sts.
Work 14 rows stocking st in stripes of 6 rows C2, 2 rows C1 and 6 rows C2.
Shape top: Using C1, dec at each end of next 2 rows.
Using C2, dec at each end of next 2 rows.
7 sts.
Cast off.
Join underarm seams.

PAWS (4)

Using Hook and C1, make 2ch.
1st Round: Miss 1ch, 6dc in next ch. (Do not join.)
2nd Round: 2dc in each of next 6dc, sl st in next dc.
Fasten off, leaving an end 15cm long to sew to arms and legs.

TO MAKE UP:

Fill head firmly, then sew ears to shaped part of seams. Fill muzzle and sew in position. Embroider features as pictured. Fill body and legs. Fill arms and sew to body. Sew head to body. Sew paws to arms and legs. To make crib string, thread several bears onto elastic with bells in between each bear. Tie 50cm of ribbon onto each end of elastic.

STORK COAT HANGER ▷

Note: Before commencing it is essential to first check your tension (see below)

YARN REQUIREMENTS:	
Villawool 3 Ply Baby (20g) Balls	1

Abbreviations: See page 125.
Accessories: 3mm (No. 10-11) crochet hook or SIZE NEEDED TO GIVE CORRECT TENSION. Small coat hanger, padded and covered; yellow and black stranded thread; tiny baby doll; ribbon.
Tension: 24.5tr and 13.75 rows to 10cm over treble fabric, using 3mm hook.

HANGER (make 2 pieces)

Make 5ch, join with a sl st to form ring.
1st Round: 3ch, 11tr in ring, sl st in 3rd ch at beg.
2nd Round: 3ch, 1tr in next tr, 2tr in next tr, (1 tr in each of next 2tr, 2tr in next tr) 3 times, sl st in 3rd ch at beg.
16tr, counting 3ch as 1tr.
3rd Round: 3ch, 1tr in each tr to end, sl st in 3rd ch at beg.
Rep 3rd round 11 times, turn.
15th Round: Working from wrong side, * insert hook in next tr, (take yarn over hook and around 1st and 2nd fingers of left hand) 4 times, yoh and draw through loops on finger, yoh and draw through all rem loops, 1dc in next tr, rep from * to end, sl st in first st, turn.
8 loops.
16th Round: 3ch, 1tr in each st to end, sl st in 3rd ch at beg.
16tr.
Rep 15th and 16th rounds 3 times, then 15th round once. Fasten off.
Slip 2 pieces over covered hanger and join at centre.

TO COVER HOOK AND MAKE HEAD

Make 6ch.
1st Row: Miss 1ch, 1dc in each ch to end.
5dc.
2nd Row: (1dc, 1ch) in first dc, 1tr in each dc to end.
3rd Row: (1dc, 1ch) in first tr, 1tr in each tr to end, 1tr in top of turning ch.
Rep 3rd row 4 times.
8th Row: (1dc, 1ch) in first tr, 2tr in each tr to end, 1tr in top of turning ch.
8tr, counting turning ch as 1tr.
Rep 3rd row 3 times.
12th Row: 1ch, 1dc in first tr, (miss 1tr, 1dc in next tr) 3 times, 1dc in top of turning ch.
13th Row: 1ch, 1dc in each dc to end.
Rep 13th row once (beak).
Fasten off.
Place over hook and join edges.
Wind yellow stranded thread firmly around dc to form beak. Embroider 2 eyes using black thread.

DOLL'S BASKET

Make 6ch, join with a sl st to form ring.
1st Round: 3ch, 16tr in ring, sl st in 3rd ch at beg.
2nd Round: 3ch, 1tr in each of next 2tr, 2tr in next tr, (1tr in each of next 3tr, 2tr in next tr) 3 times, sl st in 3rd ch at beg.
3rd Round: 3ch, 1tr in each of next 3tr, 2tr in next tr, (1tr in each of next 4tr, 2tr in next tr) 3 times, sl st in 3rd ch at beg.
4th Round (handles): 30ch, miss 6tr, sl st across next 6tr, 30ch, miss 6tr, sl st in next tr. Fasten off.
Stitch doll into basket, sew handles to hanger as illustrated. Tie a bow around base of hook.

WHITE ANKLE STRAP BOOTEES ▽

Note: Before commencing it is essential to first check your tension (see below)

MEASUREMENTS			
Age (approx)	MONTHS	3	6
Fits foot	CM	8	9.5
	INS	3.25	3.75
YARN REQUIREMENTS			
Patons Fairytale 3 Ply (50g) Balls		½	½
Or **Patons Baby Wool 3 Ply** or **3 Ply Feathersoft** (25g) Balls		1	1

Abbreviations: See page 125.
Accessories: Fairytale: 1 pr 2.75mm (No. 12); **Baby Wool** or **Feathersoft**: 1 pr 3mm (No. 11) or SIZE NEEDED TO GIVE CORRECT TENSION. 2 buttons.
Tension: 33 sts and 43 rows to 10cm over stocking stitch, using 2.75mm needles for Fairytale or 3mm needles for Baby Wool or Feathersoft.
To achieve the desired effect, these bootees have been designed to be worked on smaller needles at a tighter tension than usually recommended.

BOOTEES (beg at sole)
Cast on 35 (45) sts.
1st Row: K1, * y fwd, K16 (21), y fwd, K1, rep from * once.
2nd and Alt Rows: K1, purl to last st, K1.
3rd Row: K1, * y fwd, K18 (23), y fwd, K1, rep from * once.
5th Row: K1, * y fwd, K20 (25), y fwd, K1, rep from * once.
7th Row: K1, * y fwd, K22 (27), y fwd, K1, rep from * once.
9th Row: K1, * y fwd, K24 (29), y fwd, K1, rep from * once.
55 (65) sts.
10th Row: As 2nd row.
11th Row: Knit.
Rep 10th and 11th rows 3 (4) times.
Next Row: K1, P11 (13), K31 (37), P11 (13), K1.
Next Row: Knit.
Next Row: K1, P11 (13), K31 (37), P11 (13), K1.

SHAPE INSTEP
1st Row: K33 (38), sl 1 knitways, K1, psso, turn.
2nd Row: P12, P2 tog, turn.
3rd Row: K12, sl 1 knitways, K1, psso, turn.
Rep 2nd and 3rd rows 7 (10) times, then 2nd row once.
Next Row: Knit to end.
37 (41) sts.
Next Row: K1, P11 (13), cast off 13 sts knitways, P11 (13), K1.
Work 6 rows on last 12 (14) sts.
Cast off.
Join yarn to rem sts and work other side to correspond.

STRAP
Cast on 39 (43) sts.
Knit 2 rows garter st (1st row is wrong side).
3rd Row: K3, y fwd K2 tog (buttonhole), knit to end.
Knit 1 row. Cast off.

TO MAKE UP:
DO NOT PRESS FAIRYTALE OR FEATHERSOFT. With a slightly damp cloth and warm iron, press BABY WOOL lightly. Using a flat seam, join leg and foot seams. Sew straps in position, placing end without buttonhole to left edge of left bootee and right edge of right bootee. Sew on buttons.

GREEN AND WHITE BOOTEES ▽

Note: Before commencing it is essential to first check your tension (see below)			
MEASUREMENTS			
Age (approx)	MONTHS	3	6
Fits foot	CM	8	9.5
	INS	3.25	3.75
YARN REQUIREMENTS:			
Patons Fairytale 4 Ply or **Patonyle 4 Ply** (50g) Balls			
Main colour (MC)		½	½
Contrast (C)		Small quantity	
or Patons 4 Ply Feathersoft (25g) Balls			
Main colour (MC)		1	1
Contrast (C)		Small quantity	

Fabric from Laura Ashley

Abbreviations: See page 125.
Accessories: 1 pr 3.25mm (No. 10) knitting needles or THE REQUIRED SIZE TO GIVE CORRECT TENSION; ribbon.
Tension: 29sts and 38.5 rows to 10cm over stocking stitch using 3.25mm needles.

BOOTEES (beg at sole)
Using M, cast on 31 (39) sts.
1st Row: K1, * y fwd, K14 (18), y fwd, K1, rep from * once.
2nd and Alt Rows: K1, purl to last st, K1.
3rd Row: K1, * y fwd, K16 (20), y fwd, K1, rep from * once.
5th Row: K1, * y fwd, K18 (22), y fwd, K1, rep from * once.
7th Row: K1, * y fwd, K20 (24), y fwd, K1, rep from * once.
9th Row: K1, * y fwd, K22 (26), y fwd, K1, rep from * once.
51 (59) sts.
10th Row: As 2nd row.
** Using C, knit 4 rows garter st.
Using M, work 4 rows stocking st (working K1 at each end of purl rows). **
Using C, knit 4 rows garter st.
Break off C.

SHAPE INSTEP
Using M, **23rd Row:** K30 (34), sl 1 knitways, K1, psso, turn.
24th Row: P10, P2 tog, turn.
25th Row: K10, sl 1, K1, psso, turn.
26th Row: As 24th row.
Using C, **27th, 28th, 29th and 30th Rows:** As 25th row.
Using M, **31st Row:** As 25th row.
Rep rows 24 to 30 incl once.
Break off C.
Using M, **39th Row:** Knit to end.
35 (43) sts.
40th Row: K1, purl (inc (dec) 2 sts evenly across) to last st, K1.
37 (41) sts.
41st Row: K1, * y fwd, K2 tog, rep from * to end.
42nd Row: K1, purl to last st, K1.
Rep from ** to ** twice.
Using C, knit 3 rows garter st.
Cast off.

TO MAKE UP:
DO NOT PRESS. Using a flat seam, join leg and foot seams. Thread ribbon through holes at ankles.

◁ BABY'S OR TODDLER'S COLLAR

Note: Before commencing it is essential to first check your tension (see below)		
SIZE	**Baby**	**Toddler**
Age (approx)	3-12 months	2-4 years
YARN REQUIREMENTS:		
Patons Gem 4 Ply (50g) Balls	1	1

Abbreviations: See page 125.
Additional abbreviations below.
Accessories: 1 pr 2.75mm (No. 12) knitting needles or SIZE NEEDED TO GIVE CORRECT TENSION.
4 buttons.
Additional Abbreviations: "M2" = (y fwd) twice (thus making 2 sts).
Tension: 29 sts and 38.5 rows to 10cm over stocking st, using 2.75mm needles.

COLLAR (beg at neck edge)
Cast on 67 (71) sts.
1st Row: K6, * P1, K1, rep from * to last 5 sts, K5.
2nd Row: K5, * P1, K1, rep from * to last 4 sts, K4.
3rd Row: K2, y fwd, K2 tog (buttonhole), K2, * P1, K1, rep from * to last 5 sts, K5.
Rep 2nd row once, then 1st and 2nd rows once, inc 10 sts evenly across rib section in last row.
77 (81) sts, 6 rows rib in all.
7th Row: Knit.
8th and Alt Rows: K5, purl to last 5 sts, K5.
9th Row: K7, * y fwd, K4, rep from * to last 2 sts, K2.
94 (99) sts.
11th Row: Knit.
13th Row: K7, * y fwd, K5, rep from * to last 2 sts, K2.
111 (117) sts.
15th Row: K2, y fwd, K2 tog, knit to end.
17th Row: K8, * y fwd, K6, rep from * to last st, K1.
128 (135) sts.
19th Row: Knit.
21st Row: K8, * y fwd, K7, rep from * to last st, K1.
145 (153) sts.
23rd Row: Knit. ▷

25th Row: K9, * y fwd, K8, rep from * to end.
162 (171) sts.
27th Row: As 15th row.
29th Row: K9, * y fwd, K9, rep from * to end.
179 (189) sts.
31st Row: Knit.
33rd Row: K10, * y fwd, K10, rep from * ending last rep with K9 instead of K10.
196 (207) sts.
35th Row: Knit.
37th Row: K10, * y fwd, K11, rep from * ending last rep with K10 instead of K11.
213 (225) sts.
39th Row: As 15th row.
4 buttonholes.
40th Row: P4 (5), * (P2 tog, P5) 1 (2) time/s, (P2 tog, P4) 2 (1) time/s, rep from * to end.
180 (192) sts.
Cast on 7 sts for **Edging**.
1st Row: K7, turn.
2nd Row: Sl 1, K2, y fwd, K2 tog, "M2", K2.
3rd Row: K3, P1, K2, y fwd, (K2 tog) twice (last K2 tog uses one st of edging and one st of collar), turn.
4th Row: Sl 1, K2, y fwd, K2 tog, knit to end.
5th Row: K6, y fwd, (K2 tog) twice, turn.
6th Row: Sl 1, K2, y fwd, K2 tog, "M2", K2 tog, "M2", K2.
7th Row: K3, (P1, K2) twice, y fwd, (K2 tog) twice, turn.
8th Row: As 4th row.
9th Row: K9, y fwd, (K2 tog) twice, turn.
10th Row: Sl 1, K2, y fwd, K2 tog, ("M2", K2 tog) 3 times, K1.
11th Row: K3, (P1, K2) 3 times, y fwd, (K2 tog) twice, turn.
12th Row: As 4th row.
13th Row: Cast off 8 sts, K4, y fwd, (K2 tog) twice, turn.
Rep rows 2 to 13 incl until all collar sts have been worked off. Cast off.
TO MAKE UP:
With a slightly damp cloth and warm iron, press lightly, taking care not to flatten patt. Sew on buttons.

PAPER BADGE

Black and white newspaper photograph
Coloured transparent Contact
Safety pin
Craft glue

Cut out black and white photograph or picture and cover both sides with Contact. Trim.

Glue or sticky tape safety pin to back of picture.

PASTA BADGE

Plastic name badge
Uncooked pasta
Paint
Glitter
Craft glue

Glue pasta to plastic name badge in desired pattern. Paint and sprinkle with glitter.

CHIPS BADGE

1 empty potato chip packet
A safety pin
Non-stick oven tray

Children should be supervised by an adult when making this badge.

Place empty chip packet on non-stick oven tray. Turn oven to moderate (180 degree) heat. Place tray into oven and check progress regularly. The packets only take one to two minutes to shrink.

Pierce one corner of shrunk bag with a safety pin for pinning to jacket or shirt.

LOLLYPOP BADGE

Small round badge
Flat round lollypop
Clear varnish or nail varnish
Craft glue

Coat lollypop with varnish. When dry, glue to badge.

Badges by Karen Harborow

Jacket from Worn Out West, Paddington

STAR BROOCH

1 square black felt
1 packet glass beads
Beading needle (if stitching)
Craft glue (if gluing)
Polyester fibre fill
Large safety pin

Enlarge star shape from diagram below referring to page 125 for method. Cut two stars. Stitch or glue beads onto one star, using as many or as few as you like. Beads can be stitched or glued but stitching will last longer. When attaching lots of beads, stitch three or four at a time.

Topstitch star shapes together, leaving a space for filling. Insert fibre fill and stitch gap closed. Stitch safety pin to back of star.

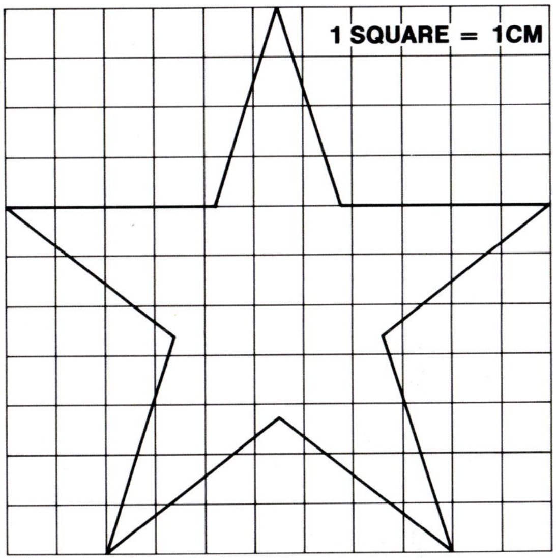

BEADED BROOCH

Felt
Cardboard
Contrasting beads
Contrasting thread
Drop pearl or button (for centre)
Small safety pin
Craft glue

Draw shape onto cardboard using picture as a guide and cut out. Use cardboard as pattern to trace onto felt and cut two shapes. Cut the felt shapes about 2mm larger than the cardboard.

On one piece of felt sew scattered beads. Glue felt shapes to either side of the cardboard shape with the beads on the outside. Topstitch around edge with contrasting thread, stitch pearl or button into centre so that it hangs down and stitch safety pin to back.

BABY'S COAT HANGER COVER△

Note: Before commencing it is essential to first check your tension (see below)

YARN REQUIREMENTS:

Patons Patonyle 4 Ply or **Fairytale 4 Ply** (50g) Balls	1
or **Patons 4 Ply Feathersoft** (25g) Balls	1

Abbreviations: See page 125.
Accessories: 1 pr 3.25mm (No. 10) knitting needles or SIZE NEEDED TO GIVE CORRECT TENSION; embroidery thread in colours of your choice; child's wooden coat hanger 30.5cm long; wadding; ribbon.
Tension: 29 sts and 38.5 rows to 10cm over stocking stitch.

COAT HANGER COVER (make 2 pieces)
Cast on 85 sts.
Knit 5 rows garter st (1st row is wrong side), inc 6 sts evenly across last row.
91 sts.
Work 26 rows stocking st.

SHAPE TOP
Cast off 9 sts at beg of next 8 rows.
Cast off rem 19 sts.

TO MAKE UP:
Using knitting stitch and six strands of embroidery thread, embroider from graphs below. See page 126 for stitch instructions.
DO NOT PRESS FAIRYTALE OR FEATHERSOFT. With a slightly damp cloth and warm iron, press PATONYLE stocking stitch lightly.
Stitch wadding onto coat hanger by hand.
Using back stitch, join side and top seams, leaving a small opening for hook. Insert hook through hole, then join lower edge seam.
Tie a bow around base of hook.

BABY'S BLOCKS▷

Note: Before commencing it is essential to first check your tension (see below)

MEASUREMENTS

Square (approx)	CM	7
	INS	2.75

YARN REQUIREMENTS
Patons Patonyle 4 Ply or Fairytale 4 Ply (50g) Balls
1 ball will make 4 Blocks or use small amounts of various colours as desired

Abbreviations: See page 125.
Accessories: 1 pair 3.25mm (No. 10) knitting needles or SIZE NEEDED TO GIVE CORRECT TENSION.
Yarn or stranded embroidery thread in colours of your choice; fibre fill or foam cubes; wooden rings.
Tension: 29 sts to 10cm in width over stocking stitch.

BLOCK
Cast on 19 sts.
Work in stocking st until work measures a square, ending with a purl row.
Cast off loosely.
Make a further 5 pieces in this manner.

TO MAKE UP:
Using knitting stitch and six strands of embroidery thread or yarn, embroider from graph below. See page 126 for stitch instructions.
DO NOT PRESS FAIRYTALE. With a slightly damp cloth and warm iron, press PATONYLE lightly.
Using back stitch, join pieces tog, having seams to outside and filling as you go or inserting foam cube.
Sew ring to block.

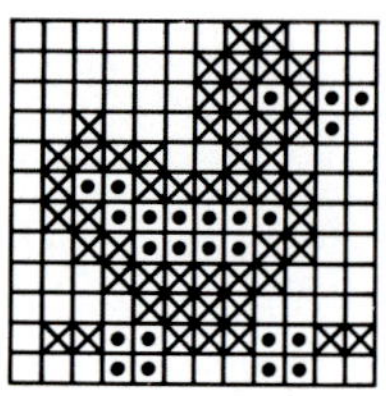

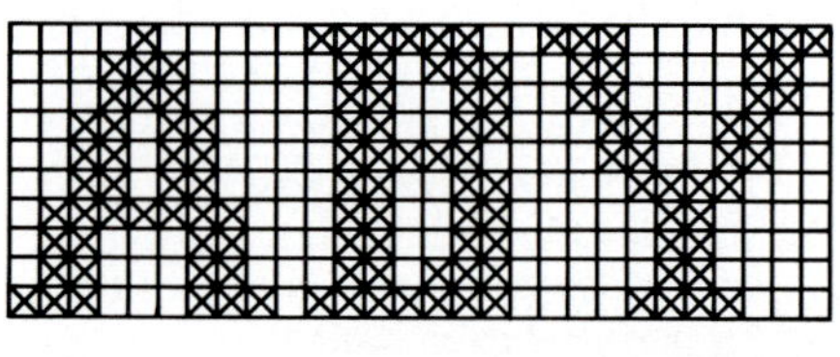

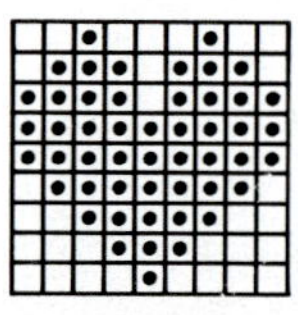

TRIMMED SINGLET AND WASHER▽

Baby singlet with lace edge
Washer
1m insertion lace
1m ribbon to fit insertion lace
50cm narrow satin ribbon

Thread ribbon through insertion lace, pin in place on washer and singlet, as desired. Machine edges to secure.

Thread narrow satin ribbon through holes at neck of singlet and tie in a bow, if desired.

Fabric from Coloroll

◁PULL-ON BIBS

Note: Before commencing it is essential to first check your tension (see below)

MEASUREMENTS		
Length	CM	24
	INS	9.5
YARN REQUIREMENTS:		
Patons Gem 4 Ply (50g) Balls		1

Abbreviations: See page 125.
Accessories: 1 pair each 2.75mm (No. 12) and 2mm (No. 14) knitting needles or SIZES NEEDED TO GIVE CORRECT TENSION; Stranded embroidery thread in colours of your choice.
Tension: 29 sts and 38.5 rows to 10cm over stocking stitch, using 2.75mm needles.

BIB
Using 2.75mm needles, cast on 59 sts.
1st Row (wrong side): Knit.
2nd Row: K2, inc in next st, knit to last 4 sts, inc in next st, K3.
Rep 1st and 2nd rows twice.
65 sts.
7th Row: K3, purl to last 3 sts, K3.
8th Row: K2, inc in next st, knit to last 4 sts, inc in next st, K3.
Rep 7th and 8th rows 3 times.
73 sts.
Work a further 57 rows stocking st, having K3 at each end of purl rows.
SHAPE NECK
Keeping garter st border correct,
Next Row: K27, cast off 19 sts, K27.
Cont on these 27 sts.
Dec at neck edge in every row 4 times, then in alt rows until 18 sts rem.
Work a further 17 rows.
SHAPE BACK NECK
Inc at neck edge in next and alt rows 3 times in all, then in every row twice.
23 sts.
Work 1 row.
Break off yarn. Leave sts on needle.
Join yarn to rem sts, P2 tog, purl to last 3 sts, K3.
Cont on these 26 sts.
Dec at neck edge in every row 3 times, then in alt rows until 18 sts rem.
Work a further 17 rows.
SHAPE BACK NECK
Inc at neck edge in next and alt rows 3 times in all, then in every row twice.
23 sts.
Work 1 row.
Next Row: K23, cast on 27 sts, knit across rem 23 sts.
73 sts.
Work a further 9 rows.
Next Row: K3, K2 tog, knit to last 5 sts, sl 1, K1, psso, K3.
Next Row: K3, purl to last 3 sts, K3.
Rep last 2 rows 4 times.
63 sts.
Next Row; K3, K2 tog, knit to last 5 sts, sl 1, K1, psso, K3.
Next Row: Knit.
Rep last 2 rows once. ▷

59 sts.
Knit 1 row.
Cast off.

NECKBAND

Using 2mm needles, cast on 117 sts.
1st Row: K2, *P1, K1, rep from * to last st, K1.
2nd Row: K1, *P1, K1, rep from * to end.
Rep 1st and 2nd rows 4 times.
10 rows rib in all.
Cast off loosely in rib.

TO MAKE UP:

Using knitting stitch and six strands of embroidery thread, embroider hearts or ducks from graph on page 50, in colours of your choice. See page 126 for stitch instructions. With a slightly damp cloth and warm iron, press stocking st lightly, Using back stitch, join ends of neckband tog, then sew cast-off edge in position around neckline.

CLARENCE THE CLOWN ▽

Note: Before commencing it is essential to first check your tension (see below)

YARN REQUIREMENTS

5 ply Knitting yarn (50g) balls

Main Colour	(white)	1½
Contrast	(red)	
	Blue	small quantity
	Black	small quantity

Abbreviations: See page 125.
Accessories: Foam ball (the size of a tennis ball); 4mm crochet hook; 35cm elastic; 25cm elastic. Fold both pieces of elastic in half; stitch together securely at the half way point to form a cross.
Tension: Each circle should measure 5cm.

BODY, ARMS, LEGS and NECK

Using main colour make 50 circles as follows.
5ch, join with a sl st in the first ch made to form a ring.
4ch, 23dtr in the ring, (24dtr altogether counting the 4ch made at the beg as 1dtr) join with a sl st in the top of the 4ch made at the beg.

HEAD

Using main colour, make 2 pieces the same. 4ch, join with a sl st in the first ch made to form a ring.
1st Round: 2ch, (these will be counted as the first st throughout this pattern) 11htr into the ring, join with a sl st in the top of the 2ch made at the beg.
12htr.
2nd Round: 2ch, 1htr in the same place as the sl st * 1htr in the next htr, 2htr in the next htr, rep from * to the last htr, 1htr in the last htr, join with a sl st in the top of 2ch made at beg.
18htr.
3rd Round: 2ch, 1htr in the same place as the sl st, * 1htr in the next htr, 2htr in the next htr, rep from the * to the last htr, 1htr in the next htr, join with a sl st in top of the 2ch made at the beg.
27htr.
4th Round: 2ch, 1htr in each htr to the end, join with a sl st in the top of 2ch made at beg.
5th Round: 2ch, 1htr in same place as sl st, * 1htr in each of the next 2htr, 2htr in the next htr, rep from *

Clown by Margaret Metcalfe

to last htr, 1htr in the next htr, join with a sl st in the top of 2ch made at the beg.
36htr.
6th Round: 2ch, 1htr in the same place as the sl st, * 1htr in each of the next 2htr, 2htr in the next htr, rep from * to last 2htr, 1htr in each of the next 2htr, join with a sl st in the top of 2ch made at the beg.
48htr.
7th Round: 2ch, 1htr in each htr to the end, join with a sl st in top of 2ch made at beg.
Fasten off.
Decorate the face (as pictured) before sewing the two pieces together over the foam ball.

HAT

Using black, 4ch, join with a sl st in the first ch made to form a ring.
1st Round: 12dc into the ring, join with a sl st in first dc made.
2nd Round: 2ch, 1htr in each dc to the end, join with a sl st in top of 2ch made at the beg.
3rd Round: same as the 2nd.
4th Round: 3ch, 2tr in the same place as the sl st, 3tr in each st to the end, join with a sl st in top of 3ch made at beg. Fasten off.
36tr.
Sew hat in place on head.

HAIR

Using contrast yarn, make 25ch. 1dc in the 2nd ch from the hook, 1dc in each ch to the end, turn.
Make the loops as follows: *insert the hook into the first st, yoh and around the index and middle fingers of the left hand (right hand if left handed) 3 times, yoh and draw through loops on the finger, yoh and draw through all remaining loops, rep from* working into the next then each st till the end.
Fasten off.
Sew securely to the head.

LEG and ARM FRILLS

Make four frills.
Make the same as for the body circles, but don't fasten off, *1dc, between the next 2dtr, 3ch, rep from* to the end join with a sl st in the first dc made.
Fasten off.
Join in contrast colour, in any 3ch loop, 1dc in the same loop, *3ch, 1dc into the next loop, rep from* to the end, join with a sl st in first dc made.

NECK FRILL

Make the same as the leg and arm frills, with main colour, do not fasten off, continue as follows: sl st into the first 3ch loop, 1dc in the same loop, *3ch, 1dc in to the next loop, rep from* to the end, join with a sl st in the first dc made.
Fasten off main colour.
Join in contrast colour, in any 3ch loop, 1dc in the same loop. *3ch, 1dc into the next loop, rep from* to the end, join with a sl st in first dc made.

POMPOMS

Make four.
Cut 2 circles of cardboard measuring 4cm across, cut a round hole of 1cm in the centre of each, wind equal amounts of main and contrast colour yarn through centre hole and around the cardboard, till the centre is filled. With a sharp pair of scissors, place the point between the two pieces of cardboard, cut all the way around the pompom keeping the scissors between the 2 pieces of the cardboard at all times. Tie securely with a length of yarn between the cardboard, leaving the end of the yarn to sew to elastic, remove the cardboard.
Trim pompom.

TO MAKE UP:

Attach elastic securely to head. Thread 2 circles and neck frill over all ends of elastic. Thread 9 circles and arm frill over each end of the short elastic, sew pompom to the elastic securely. Thread 12 circles over both ends of the longer elastic for the body. Thread 9 circles and leg frill over each end of the long elastic, sew pompom to elastic securely.

SEASIDE CRIB STRING ▷

5 different coloured pieces of felt
70cm x 35mm green ribbon
70cm x 3mm green ribbon
1m x 15mm green ribbon
40cm elastic
Polyester fibre fill

Sea shapes. Enlarge patterns below following method on page 125. Draw sea shapes onto doubled felt and cut out. (Cut out crab shape after sewing.) Sew fabric together leaving a gap. Insert polyester filling, stitch to close gap. ▷

1 SQUARE = 1CM

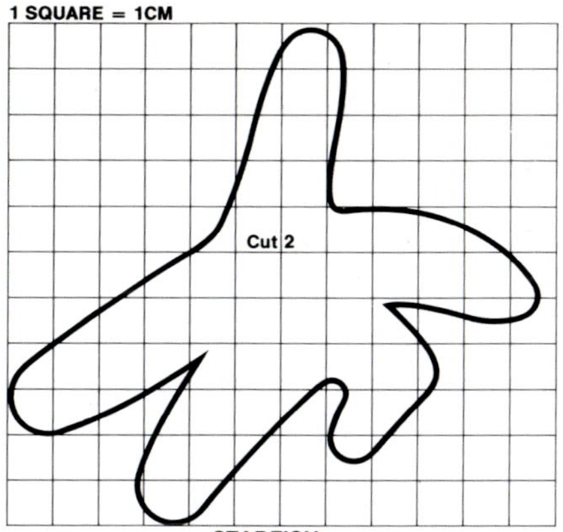

STARFISH

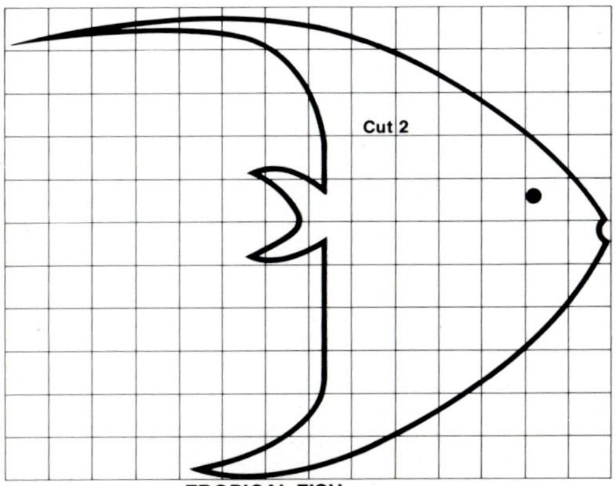

TROPICAL FISH

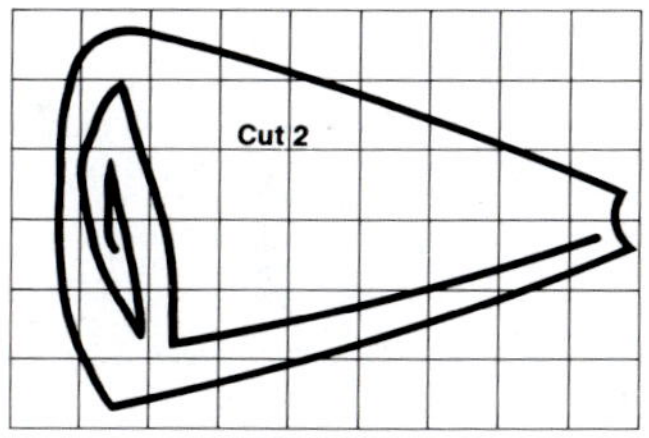

CONE SHELL

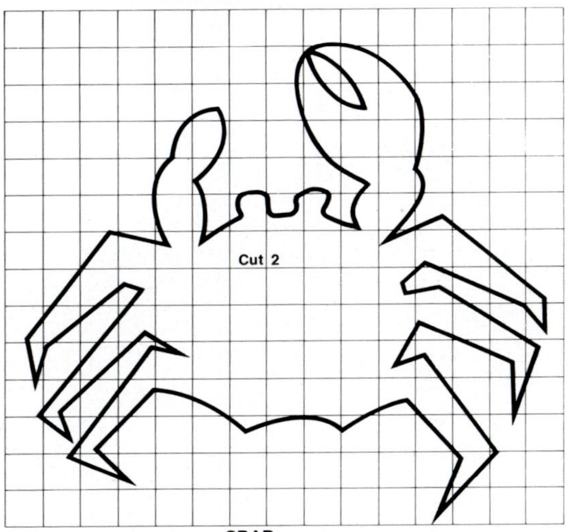

CRAB

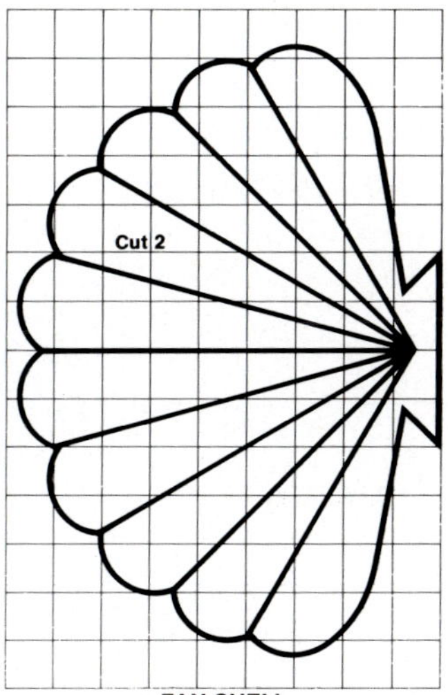

FAN SHELL

Stitch detail on shells by sewing straight lines. Add 2 or 3 hand stitches for fish eyes.

Crib string. Fold 35mm ribbon right sides together lengthwise, and sew, turn right way out using a safety pin and thread elastic through ribbon. Stitch each end. Ribbon should be gathered over elastic at this stage. Cut 15mm ribbon length in half and attach each piece to the end of ribbon/elastic strip; these will form the ties for the mobile.

Cut the 3mm ribbon into varying lengths. Sew the shorter pieces to the shells and the longer lengths to the remaining shapes. Make a bow where ribbon joins felt shape.

Stitch other end of ribbon to elastic ribbon positioning shapes at intervals across the crib string.

ANIMAL PENCIL CASES

Fabric scraps
Sew-on eyes
13cm zipper (1 each animal)
Scrap of ribbon (kangaroo)
Stranded embroidery thread
Fabric paint
Craft glue
Fusible interfacing

Dog. Enlarge patterns referring to page 125 for method. Cut two body shapes and four ear shapes using pattern, and adding seam allowance. Apply interfacing to body pieces.

Join one side of the zipper to one of the body pieces between the notches. Join the other side of the zipper to the other body piece in the same way. Place pairs of ears, right sides together and sew around curved edges leaving top straight edge open. Trim and clip seam and turn ears out to right side.

Pin ears in position on the body pieces. Place body pieces right sides together and sew around the seam line, making sure the ears are caught in place. Trim seams, clip curves and overlock edges. Turn animal right side out through zipper. Push out points of tail and legs with a pencil. Embroider, applique or paint the facial details as indicated on pattern pieces. Sew on or embroider eyes.

Kangaroo. Follow the instructions for the dog. Kangaroo's ears are part of the pattern and don't need to be constructed separately.

Tiger. Follow the instructions for the dog. The mouth is appliqued onto the fabric before the body pieces are joined. Embroider teeth. Use fabric paint to apply stripes.

Elephant. Follow instructions for dog. Applique tusks before stitching body pieces together.

Pencil cases by Sue Cadzow

Crib string by Jillian Morrow

1 SQ = 5CM
1 SQ = 5CM
1 SQ = 5CM

SILKY CROCHETED BOOTEES

Note: Before commencing it is essential to first check your tension (see below)

YARN REQUIREMENTS:
Rayon 3 ply (commonly called silk) 1 reel

Abbreviations: See page 125.
Accessories: 2mm and 1.25mm crochet hooks or SIZE REQUIRED TO GIVE CORRECT TENSION; 1m 6mm-wide ribbon; green and pink stranded embroidery thread; 2m of 1cm-wide lace (cut into 6 equal lengths and stitch ends to form circles of lace).
Tension: 28tr over 10cm length using above materials.
BOOTEES
Using a 2mm crochet hook, make 20ch.
1st Round: 3tr in 4th ch from the hook, 1tr in each of the next 9ch, 1dtr in each of the next 6ch, 9dtr in last ch, working along opposite side of ch, 1dtr in each of the next 6ch, 1tr in each of the next 9ch, 4tr in same place as the 3tr made at beg, join with a sl st in top of 3ch made at beg.
2nd Round: 3ch, 2tr in next tr, 1tr in the next tr, 2tr in the next tr, 1 tr in each of the next 15sts, * 2tr in the next st, 1tr in the next st, work from * 4 times in all, 2tr in next st, 1tr in each of the next 15sts, 2tr in next st, 1tr in next tr, 2tr in next tr, 1tr in the last tr, join with a sl st in the top of 3ch made at the beg.
56tr altogether.
3rd and 4th Rounds: 3ch, 1tr in each tr to the end, join with a sl st in the top of 3ch made at beg.
5th Round: Change to a 1.25mm crochet hook, with right side facing and 1 circle of lace, insert hook through lace and same place as sl st make 1dc, * insert hook through lace and next st, make 1dc, evenly easing the lace as you work, rep from * to end, join with a sl st in first dc made.
6th Round: Change to a 2mm crochet hook, work same as 3rd round.
Rep 5th and 6th rounds once, then the 5th round once.
56dc in total.
10th Round: 1dc in the same place as the sl st, 1dc in each of the next 33sts, miss next st, sl st across the next 2dc, turn.
Next Row: Miss the 2 sl st, 1tr in each of the next 10sts, miss the next st, sl st across the next 2sts, turn.
Rep last row 4 times.
Next Row: Miss the 2 sl st, 1tr in each of the next 10tr, 1dc in each st to the end, join with a sl st in the first dc made on the 10th round.
Next Round: Work ribbon holes as follows, 4ch, * miss 1 stitch, 1tr in next st, 1ch, rep from * to end, join with a sl st in 3rd of the 4ch made at beg.
Next Round: Sl st into the first 1ch space, (3ch, 1tr, 2ch, 2tr) in same space, miss one 1ch space, * (2tr, 2ch, 2tr) in next space, miss 1 space, rep from * to end, join with a sl st in top of 3ch made at beg.
Next Round: Sl st into the first 2ch space, 1dc in same space, 5ch, * 1dc into next 2ch space, 5ch, rep from * ending with a sl st in the first dc made at the beg.
Last Round: (3dc, 3ch, sl st into the last dc made, 3dc) into each 5ch loop till the end, sl st into the first dc made at the beg.
Fasten off.
TO MAKE UP:
Thread ribbon through ribbon holes. Using six strands of embroidery thread, work grub (bullion) roses in pink and green as pictured. See page 126 for bullion stitch instructions.

SILKY CROCHETED BIB

Note: Before commencing it is essential to first check your tension (see below)

YARN REQUIREMENTS:
Rayon 3 ply (commonly called silk) 1 reel

Abbreviations: See page 125.
Accessories: 2mm crochet hook or SIZE REQUIRED TO GIVE CORRECT TENSION; 1m of 6mm-wide ribbon; green and pink stranded embroidery thread.
Tension: 6 shells over 10cm using above materials.
BIB
Make 71ch.
1dc into the 2nd ch from the hook, 1dc in each ch to the end.
Fasten off.
1st Row: Join yarn into the 25th dc from the beginning, 3ch, * miss 2dc, (3tr, 1ch, 3tr) into the next dc, * repeat from * to * 5 times, (6 shells made) miss 2dc, 1tr into the next dc, turn.
2nd Row: 3ch, * (3tr, 1ch, 3tr) into the next 1ch space of the shell * rep from * to * to end, 1tr into top of 3ch, turn.
Repeat 2nd row 4 times.
7th Row: Sl st into each st to the first 1ch space of shell, 3ch, * into the next 1ch space of shell work

Bib and bootees by Margaret Metcalfe.

(3tr, 1ch, 3tr) rep from * 3 times, 3ch, 1dc into the 1ch space of the last shell.
4 shells made.
8th Row: Sl st into each st to the first 1ch space of shell, 3ch, * into the next 1ch space of shell work (3tr, 1ch, 3tr) rep from * once, 3ch, 1dc, into the 1ch space of last shell.
2 shells.
Fasten off.
Rejoin yarn to the beginning of the dc row, 3ch, then work 1tr in each dc, then work 77tr evenly around the shell area, then 1tr in each of the remaining dc, turn.
125tr made.
Next Row: Make ribbon holes as follows, 5ch, miss 1tr, * 1dtr in next tr, 1ch, miss 1tr, rep from * till end working the last dtr in top of the 3ch, turn.
Next Row: 3ch, * 1tr into the next 1ch space, 1tr into the next dtr, * rep from * to * 24 times, then work 2tr in each 1ch space and 1tr in each dtr, till 25 1ch spaces remain. Rep from * working the last tr in the 4th of the 5ch, turn.
Next Row: * 3ch, miss 1tr, 1dc into the next tr, rep from * to the end. Turn.
Last Row: * 1dc into the next 3ch loop, 3ch, 1dc into the same loop. Rep from * to the end. Fasten off.
TO MAKE UP:
Thread ribbon through ribbon holes leaving enough ribbon at the neck edges to tie a bow.
Using six strands of embroidery thread, work grub (bullion) roses in pink and green as pictured. See page 126 for bullion stitch instructions.

FOOD for SALE

We have selected a delicious array of homemade treats, all sure to be fete favourites. To increase stall profits, sell sweets by the piece and pies and cakes by the slice. Finishing touches are important too. Label jars, tie pretty ribbon bows on bottles and package sweets in cellophane wrap. Why not double the fete fun by holding a sweet lucky dip!

RIGHT: Lemonade (recipe overpage).

Props used in food photography from Appley Hoare Antiques, Mosman; Home and Garden, Sydney; Ditz, Newtown.

LEMONADE
4
SALE 20¢

◁LEMONADE

Set up a stall just for lemonade, it will be popular on a hot day.

2 cups sugar
1 cup water
1 cup lemon juice

Combine the sugar and water in a pan, bring to the boil, stirring until sugar is dissolved. Boil gently for 5 minutes without stirring. Cool, then add lemon juice.

Strain and store in refrigerator until ready to serve. When ready to serve add 2 tablespoons syrup to 1 glass iced water. You can mix jugs of lemonade and decorate with extra slices of lemon or sprigs of mint.

Multiply quantities depending on the amount you wish to make.

ALMOND CAKE▽

This is a moist cake that will keep well in an airtight container or will freeze for up to 2 months.

185g butter
1 cup sugar
½ teaspoon vanilla essence
3 eggs
3 cups self-raising flour
1 cup ground almonds
¾ cup milk
½ cup whole blanched almonds
¼ cup glace cherries

Cream butter and sugar until light and fluffy. Add vanilla, beat well. Add eggs one at a time and beat well after each addition. Sift flour and fold into mixture with the ground almonds and milk. Pour mixture into a greased and lined deep sided 20cm cake pan.

Press the whole almonds and cherries into the top of the mixture to form flowers. Bake in a moderate oven 1 hour or until cake is cooked when tested. Allow to cool on a wire rack.

TOMATO RELISH▷

Bottle your relish attractively and label, including the date made.

4kg ripe tomatoes
1½kg onions
2 tablespoons dry mustard
2 tablespoons curry paste
1½kg sugar
375ml bottle Ezy-sauce
½ cup flour
½ cup water

Blanch tomatoes and remove skin, chop finely, chop onions finely. Combine tomatoes, onions, mustard and curry powder in a large saucepan; place over moderate heat and bring to the boil.

Add sugar and Ezy-sauce and boil approximately 2½ hours. Mix the flour and water to a smooth paste and stir into the relish, continue cooking until thickened. Pour hot relish into sterilised jars, allow to cool slightly and seal. Label bottles.

MAYONNAISE △

Homemade mayonnaise is very simple to make, adjust the seasonings to suit your taste, or add a flavour that you particularly enjoy; French mustard, chives or herbs.

2 egg yolks
½ teaspoon salt
pinch white pepper
½ teaspoon dry mustard
2 teaspoons lemon juice or vinegar
1 cup oil

Have all ingredients at room temperature. Place egg yolks, seasonings and 1 teaspoon of lemon juice or vinegar in a bowl and whisk to combine. When thick add the oil drop by drop, whisking constantly and incorporating each addition of oil before adding the next.

As the mixture thickens the oil flow may be increased to a steady thin stream. Keep whisking constantly. When all oil is incorporated beat in the remaining lemon juice or vinegar.

If mixture should show signs of curdling add 2 teaspoons boiling water before continuing adding the oil.

Mayonnaise may be made successfully in the food processor, however the texture will be slightly different.

Makes approximately 1 cup.

LEFT: Almond Cake.
ABOVE: From left: Tomato Relish, Mayonnaise.

TOFFEE APPLES

Toffee apples are always a great attraction at fetes, why not set up a toffee apple stand and cook them to order. You can use an electric deep fryer to make the toffee. The skewers can be bought from your local butcher.

40 crisp red apples
2kg sugar
2¼ cups water
½ cup vinegar
½ teaspoon cream of tartar
½ teaspoon red or green food colouring

Wash apples and dry thoroughly. Place sugar, water, vinegar and cream of tartar into deep fryer or pan with temperature set at 150°C. Stir until sugar is dissolved. Leave to boil for approximately 15 minutes.

Lightly grease a few baking trays. Add the food colouring to the toffee then quickly dip the skewered apples into the toffee. Allow the excess toffee to drip back into the pan and place the apples on the trays to set.

POPCORN

Popcorn is very easy to make and can look terrific packaged in bags.

1 cup popcorn kernels
30g butter
1 teaspoon salt

Heat the butter in a heavy based pan, add the popcorn and cook over a medium heat with the lid on. Shake the pan every now and then and do not lift lid until popping has stopped.

Sprinkle with salt, allow to cool and package in bags tied with ribbon.

LEFT: From left: Popcorn, Toffee Apples.

LEFT: Berry Sponge (recipe overpage).

◁BERRY SPONGE

This sponge cake will freeze well for up to 2 months; add berries and icing sugar just prior to serving.

3 eggs
¾ cup castor sugar
1 cup self-raising flour
1 punnet strawberries
other seasonal berries if desired
icing sugar

Separate eggs, beat egg whites until stiff peaks form. Add sugar gradually, beating until sugar is dissolved. Add egg yolks and beat until combined. Fold through sifted flour gently. Place in a greased and lined ring pan and bake in a moderate oven 30 minutes or until cake springs back when touched.

Turn onto a wire rack to cool. Dress with assorted berries and dust with icing sugar.

FIG LOAF△

This is a moist loaf that will keep well, or can be frozen for up to 2 months.

2 cups dessert figs, chopped
2 tablespoons sugar
30g butter
½ cup water, boiling
2 cups self-raising flour
1 teaspoon bi-carbonate of soda
1 egg

Place the figs, sugar and butter in a bowl and cover with the boiling water. Allow to cool. Sift the flour and soda together. Fold flour and egg into fig mixture and place into 2 greased and lined small loaf pans.

Bake approximately 40 minutes in a moderate oven or until cooked when tested.

CREAMY COCONUT ICE ▽

This is a simple uncooked version of the popular coconut ice. Cut into squares and wrap in cellophane.

2½ cups icing sugar
2½ cups coconut
1 teaspoon vanilla
2 egg whites
125g copha

In a bowl combine sifted icing sugar, coconut, vanilla and egg whites. Melt copha over a gentle heat; it should be barely warm, not hot. Combine with dry ingredients.

Press half mixture into a lamington pan, colour the remaining half of mixture to a delicate pink using food colouring and press onto white mixture. Sprinkle top with a little extra coconut, if desired, and refrigerate until set. Cut into squares to serve.

LEFT: Fig Loaf.
BELOW: Creamy Coconut Ice.
RIGHT: Pikelets.

PIKELETS △

Pikelets are best eaten warm with jam and cream. They may be reheated successfully in the microwave.

1 cup self-raising flour
1 tablespoon sugar
½ cup milk
1 egg
butter for greasing pan

Sift the flour and sugar, whisk in the beaten egg and milk. Mixture should be slightly lumpy. Lightly grease and heat a skillet and drop spoonfuls of mixture onto skillet.

Turn when brown underneath and when bubbles appear through the mixture.

Cook second side. Continue until all mixture is used. It may be easier to cook 3 at a time.

Makes approximately 2 dozen.

PECAN CINNAMON PIE ▽

Pecan pie may be served hot or cold with whipped cream. Pie will keep refrigerated for 3 days.

PASTRY
1½ cups flour
90g butter
3 tablespoons iced water
FILLING
3 eggs
1 cup corn syrup
1 cup sugar
60g butter, melted
1 teaspoon cinnamon
1½ cups pecans

To prepare pastry sift flour, rub in butter using fingertips. Add water and mix to a dough using a knife. Press together using hands. Knead lightly and roll out on a lightly floured surface to fit an 18cm pie dish. Trim edge and pinch with fingertips to form a fluted edge.

Whisk together the eggs, corn syrup, sugar, butter and cinnamon. Fold the pecans through the syrup mixture and pour into pastry case. Bake in a moderate oven 50-55 minutes or until a knife inserted in the centre of the pie comes out clean. Dust with icing sugar when cool, if desired.

GEM SCONES ▷

Gem scone pans (irons) are usually constructed from cast iron to hold the heat, they are well worth having as gem scones are a quick and delicious treat.

30g butter
1½ tablespoons sugar
1 egg
1 cup milk
1½ cups self-raising flour

Mix the butter and sugar together, add the egg and cream the mixture. Add the milk and sifted flour and mix lightly. The mixture should be thick and able to drop from a spoon.

Have the irons hot and buttered. Spoon mixture into irons and bake in a hot oven 5 minutes or until golden brown.

Makes approximately 15.

BELOW: Pecan Cinnamon Pie.
RIGHT: Gem Scones.

namco
GEM
SCONES

COOKIES

GINGERNUTS

These are crisp biscuits that freeze well for up to 2 months.

2 cups flour
1 cup castor sugar
½ teaspoon bi-carbonate of soda
1 teaspoon cinnamon
2 teaspoons ground ginger
125g butter
1 egg
1 teaspoon golden syrup

Sift flour, sugar, soda, cinnamon and ginger into a bowl. Rub in butter using fingertips. Add the egg and golden syrup to dry ingredients and work to a firm dough.

Place teaspoons of mixture on lightly greased oven trays about 5cm apart. Bake in a moderately slow oven approximately 15 minutes. Allow biscuits to cool on trays.

Makes about 40 biscuits.

FRUIT COOKIES

These cookies will freeze for up to 2 months.

¾ cup self-raising flour
1 cup dried fruit medley
1 cup cornflakes
1 cup coconut
½ cup sugar
125g butter
1 tablespoon honey
1 egg

Sift flour and combine in a bowl with other dry ingredients. Melt butter and honey and add to dry ingredients with the egg. Mix well.

Drop spoonfuls of mixture onto lightly greased oven trays and bake in a moderate oven for 12 minutes or until golden brown. Allow to cool on trays.

Makes approximately 24.

LEFT: From top: Gingernuts, Fruit Cookies.
BELOW: Kiflice (recipe overpage).

◁KIFLICE

A Yugoslavian sweet pastry that is filled with walnuts or plum powidl, a thick plum jam that is available in delicatessens.

250g self-raising flour
60g butter
150mls cream
200g walnuts
4 tablespoons sugar
1 tablespoon hot milk

Rub butter into flour using fingertips. Using a knife, mix the cream into the flour mixture to form a dough. Roll the dough out on a lightly floured surface to 5mm thickness. Using a bread and butter plate as a guide cut circles from the dough. Cut each circle into 6 triangles.

Grind the walnuts in a blender or with a rolling pin. Add the sugar and add drops of hot milk until mixture holds together. Place a small amount of walnut mixture on the larger end of each triangle. Roll the triangle into a crescent shape to enclose walnut mixture. Walnuts may be replaced with plum jam.

Place on a greased baking tray and bake in a moderate oven 10 minutes or until golden brown. Roll in icing sugar while still hot.

Makes approximately 30.

CHEESE PLAITS▷

Serve these warm or cold, they are best made just prior to the fete.

1 packet ready rolled puff pastry
250g tasty cheese

Cut each sheet of pastry into thin strips. Grate the cheese. Take three strips of pastry and pinch together at one end. Plait the pastry and join at the other end. Continue until all of the pastry has been plaited.

Place the plaits on lightly greased oven trays and sprinkle with the grated cheese. Bake in a moderately hot oven 7 minutes or until pastry is puffed and golden brown. Place onto wire racks to cool.

Makes approximately 40.

RIGHT: Cheese Plaits.

PASSIONFRUIT SPONGE ▷

A light, easy sponge recipe that is layered with whipped cream and topped with passionfruit icing. This cake is best eaten fresh.

3 eggs
¾ cup castor sugar
1 cup self-raising flour
3 tablespoons boiling water
300ml carton thickened cream
2 tablespoons icing sugar
½ teaspoon vanilla essence
ICING
½ cup icing sugar
2 passionfruit
1 teaspoon butter

Separate eggs, beat egg whites until stiff. Add sugar gradually, continue beating until sugar is dissolved. Beat in egg yolks. Sift flour and fold into egg mixture with boiling water. Fold gently and quickly. Pour mixture into 3 greased and lined sandwich pans and bake in a moderate oven 15 minutes or until cake springs back when touched. Turn cakes onto a wire rack to cool.

Whip the cream with icing sugar and vanilla. Sift icing sugar and mix to an icing with the pulp from the passionfruit and the butter.

Spread half of the cream onto one cake, top with another cake and spread with the remaining cream. Top with the third cake and ice with passionfruit icing.

PASSIONFRUIT
SPONGE

APPLE SPICE CAKE△

This cake will keep well in an airtight container or can be frozen for up to 2 months.

125g butter
¾ cup castor sugar
2 eggs
2 cups self-raising flour
½ cup milk
1 green apple
2 tablespoons sugar, extra
1 teaspoon cinnamon
½ teaspoon mixed spice

Cream butter and sugar until light and fluffy. Add eggs one at a time and beat well. Sift flour and fold into butter mixture lightly with milk. Pour mixture into a greased and lined deep sided 20cm cake pan. Peel and slice apple thinly. Layer the apple slices on top of the cake mixture.

Combine the extra sugar, cinnamon and spice and sprinkle on top of the apple. Bake in a moderate oven 40-50 minutes or until cooked when tested. Allow to cool in pan slightly before turning onto a wire rack to cool.

LEFT: Passionfruit Sponge (recipe previous page). ABOVE: Apple Spice Cake.

AUSTRALIA

◁LAVENDER VINEGAR

This vinegar is delicately flavoured and is suitable to use in dressings. It looks particularly pretty for a fete; decorate the bottle with a little sprig of lavender and some ribbon.

1 sprig of lavender
2 tablespoons of dried lavender flowers
2 cups white vinegar

Place the dried lavender flowers in a bottle. Heat the vinegar and pour into bottle. Allow to cool and place lavender sprig into bottle. Seal and place in a dark place for 3-4 weeks before using.

Makes 2 cups.

◁HERB OIL

A bottle of herb oil makes a lovely gift and is handy to have in the pantry. Add instant flavour to your dressings, mayonnaise or pasta.

3 sprigs of any fresh herb, such as tarragon, oregano or thyme
2 cloves garlic, optional
5 peppercorns
2 cups olive oil

Place the herbs into a bottle, peel the garlic and add to the bottle with the peppercorns. Warm the oil slightly and pour into the bottle. Seal and store for 3-4 weeks before using.

Makes 2 cups.

◁CHILLI OIL

Use a few drops of this hot oil to cook with or add to dressings.

2 tablespoons dried chillies
2 cups oil

Place chillies in a bottle or jar. Warm the oil and pour over chillies. Allow to cool, seal and store for 5-6 weeks before use. Shake bottle or jar occasionally.

Makes 2 cups.

LEFT: From left: Lavender Vinegar, Herb Oil, Chilli Oil.

◁ MILLET AND LINSEED DAMPERS

Damper is best eaten fresh, preferably warm with butter. The addition of millet and linseed gives this damper a real homebaked country taste.

2½ cups self-raising flour
1 teaspoon salt
¼ cup millet
¼ cup linseed
90g butter
1 cup water
100g tasty cheese, grated
1 tablespoon sesame seeds, sunflower seeds or chives

Sift flour and combine with salt, millet and linseed. Rub in butter using fingertips. Mix to a dough using a knife while adding water. Knead lightly on a floured surface.

Cut dough in half and shape into 2 rounds. Place rounds on a baking tray and mark the tops of each damper into 6 using a knife.

Sprinkle the tops with grated cheese and sesame seeds, sunflower seeds or chives. Bake in a hot oven 25 minutes or until golden brown.

Makes 2 dampers.

LEFT: Millet and Linseed Dampers.
ABOVE: Lemon Butter (recipe overpage).

◁LEMON BUTTER

Store in the refrigerator after opening.

4 eggs
¾ cup sugar
½ cup lemon juice
¼ cup water
2 teaspoons grated lemon rind
125g butter

Whisk eggs and sugar in the top half of a double saucepan over simmering water; gradually add lemon juice and water. Add lemon rind and small pieces of the butter, continue whisking and adding the butter until mixture thickens and coats the back of a wooden spoon.

Pour into hot sterilised jars. Cool slightly then seal and label bottles.

ABOVE: Raspberry Pie.
RIGHT: Turkish Delight.

◁RASPBERRY COCONUT PIE

This pie will freeze well for up to 2 months.

¾ cup flour
½ cup self-raising flour
½ cup cornflour
90g butter
2 tablespoons castor sugar
1 egg yolk
1 tablespoon milk
¾ cup raspberry jam
1 cup coconut
2 egg whites

Sift flour, self-raising flour and cornflour together. Cream butter and sugar. Beat in the egg yolk and fold in the flour mixture to form a short dough; use the milk if necessary.

Turn onto a lightly floured board and roll to fit an 18cm flan tin. Press pastry into flan tin and trim edge. Spread jam over pastry. Mix egg whites into coconut and spread on top of jam. Bake in a moderate oven 30 minutes or until coconut is a golden brown.

TURKISH DELIGHT▷

A Middle Eastern sweet that packages well. It is delicious served with strong coffee.

2 tablespoons gelatine
1 cup water
2 tablespoons rose water
3 cups sugar
⅔ cup cornflour
red food colouring
icing sugar

Sprinkle gelatine over ¼ cup water and allow to soften. Place rose water, sugar and ⅔ cup water in a pan. Bring slowly to the boil, stirring to dissolve sugar before boiling point is reached. Boil without stirring for 4-5 minutes until a sweets thermometer reads 105°C, or when a spoon of syrup dropped in cold water forms long threads.

Mix cornflour with remaining cold water and add to the syrup with the softened gelatine. Simmer until clear and gelatine has dissolved. Stir occasionally. Add a few drops of food colouring and strain into a lightly oiled lamington pan. Allow to set overnight. Cut into squares and roll in sifted icing sugar.

GIFTS for EVERYONE

What better gift than a handmade one! Here's an adorable family of well dressed mice to crochet. On following pages take note of the innovative cards and stationery; check out new ways to cover coat hangers and be inspired by our unique buttons. There are pretty boxes to make, and a batch of travel bags which will organise the most haphazard suitcase! Don't keep these ideas for fetes alone — they'll be most appreciated as Christmas gifts.

RIGHT: Family of Mice (instructions overpage).

◁FAMILY OF MICE

Note: Before commencing it is essential to first check your tension (see below)

MEASUREMENTS

Baby mice		
Height (approx)	CM	19
	INS	7.5
Adult mice		
Height	CM	24
	INS	9.5

YARN REQUIREMENTS:

Baby mice are worked in 5 ply and adult mice are worked in 8 ply.

Villawool 5 Ply Machinewash (50g) Balls	
Grey	1
Pink	1
Green	1
Yellow	1
Brown	small quantity
White	1
Red	1

This quantity will make the 3 baby mice.

Villawool 8 Ply Machinewash (50g) Balls	
Grey	2
Pink	1
Yellow	1
Red	1
Blue	1
White	1
Green	1
Brown	small quantity

This quantity will make both the adult mice.

Abbreviations: See page 125. Additional abbreviations below.
Accessories: 3.50mm (No. 9) and 4mm (No. 8) crochet hooks, or SIZES NEEDED TO GIVE CORRECT TENSION; Polyester fibre fill.
Additional Abbreviations: "Dec A" = draw up a loop in each of next 2dc, yarn over hook and draw through 3 loops on hook; "Dec B" = draw up a loop in each of next 3dc, yarn over hook and draw through 4 loops on hook.
Tension: For baby mice; 23.5dc and 31 rows to 10cm over double crochet fabric, using 3.50mm hook. For adult mice; 19dc and 23 rows to 10cm over double crochet fabric, using 4mm hook. If less sts use smaller hook, if more sts use bigger hook.

GIRL MOUSE WITH PINK JUMPER

BODY (beg at lower edge):
Using 3.50mm hook and pink, make 2ch.
1st Row: (right side): Miss 1ch, 7dc in 2nd ch.
2nd Row: 1ch, 1dc in first dc, 2dc in each of next 2dc, 1dc in next dc, 2dc in each of next 2dc, 1dc in last dc.
11dc.
3rd Row: 1ch, 1dc in first dc, 2dc in each of next 4dc, 1dc in next dc, 2dc in each of next 4dc, 1dc in last dc.
19dc.
4th Row: 1ch, (1dc in next dc, 2dc in next dc) 4 times, 1dc in each of next 3dc, (2dc in next dc, 1dc in next dc) 4 times.
27dc.
5th Row: 1ch, 1dc in each dc to end.
Rep 5th row 14 times.
20th Row: 1ch, (1dc in next dc, "Dec A") 9 times.
18dc.
21st Row: As 5th row.
22nd Row: 1ch, 1dc in first dc, ("Dec A") 8 times, 1dc in last dc.
10dc.
23rd Row: As 5th row.
24th Row: 1ch, ("Dec A") 5 times.
5dc.
25th Row: 1ch, 1dc in first dc, ("Dec A") twice.
3dc.
Fasten off.
Using a flat seam, join centre back seam, filling as you go.
HEAD (beg at neck edge):
Using 3.50mm hook and grey, make 10ch.
1st Row: (right side): Miss 1ch, 1dc in each ch to end.
9dc.
2nd Row: 1ch, 2dc in each dc to end.
18dc.
3rd Row: 1ch, 2dc in first dc, 1dc in each dc to last dc, 2dc in last dc.
4th Row: 1ch, 2dc in first dc, 1dc in each of next 4dc, (2dc in next dc, 1dc in each of next 2dc) 4 times, 1dc in each of next 2dc, 2dc in last dc.
26dc.
Rep 3rd row 3 times.
32dc.
8th Row: 1ch, 1dc in each dc to end.
9th Row: 1ch, "Dec A", 1dc in each dc to last 2dc, "Dec A".
Rep 9th row 4 times.
22dc.
14th Row: 1ch, "Dec A", (1dc in each of next 2dc, "Dec A") 5 times.
16dc.
15th Row: As 9th row.
14dc.
16th Row: 1ch, "Dec A", (1dc in next dc, "Dec A") 4 times.
9dc.
Fasten off.
Using a flat seam, join head seam filling as you go. Sew head to body.
Using brown and white, embroider face as pictured.
ARMS:
Using 3.50mm hook and grey, make 2ch.
1st Row: (right side): Miss 1ch, 7dc in 2nd ch.
2nd Row: 1ch, 1dc in first dc, (2dc in next dc, 1dc in next dc) 3 times.
10dc.
3rd Row: 1ch, 1dc in each dc to end.
Rep 3rd row 9 times, in stripes of 5 rows grey and 4 rows pink.
Fasten off.
Using a flat seam, join arm seam, filling as you go and leaving top open. Sew arms to body.
EARS:
Using 3.50mm hook and pink, make 3ch, join with a sl st to form a ring.
1st Round: 1ch, 6dc in ring, sl st in first dc.
2nd Round: 1ch, 2dc in same place as sl st, 2dc in each dc to end, sl st in first dc.
12dc.
3rd Round: 1ch, 1dc in same place as sl st, 2dc in next dc, (1dc in next dc, 2dc in next dc) 5 times, sl st in first dc.
18dc.
Fasten off.
Using grey, make another piece the same.
Hold pieces tog with wrong sides inside. With pink side facing, using grey work 1 round dc evenly around outside edge working through double thickness.
Fasten off.
Sew ears to head as illustrated.
LEGS:
Using 3.50mm hook and green, make 8ch.
1st Row: (right side): Miss 1ch, 1dc in each of next 3ch, 3dc in next ch, 1dc in each of next 3ch.
9dc.
2nd Row: 1ch, 2dc in first dc, 1dc in each of next 3dc, 3dc in next dc, 1dc in each of next 3dc, 2dc in last dc.
13dc.
3rd Row: 1ch, 2dc in first dc, 1dc in

each of next 5dc, 3dc in next dc, 1dc in each of next 5dc, 2dc in last dc.
17dc.
4th Row: 1ch, 2dc in first dc, 1dc in each dc to last dc, 2dc in last dc.
19dc.
5th Row: Working in back loops only, 1ch, 1dc in each of next 8dc, 2dc in each of next 3dc, 1dc in each of next 8dc.
22dc.
Working through both loops again,
6th Row: 1ch, 1dc in each dc to end.
7th Row: 1ch, 1dc in each of next 8dc, ("Dec A") 3 times, 1dc in each of next 8dc.
19dc.
8th Row: 1ch, 1dc in each of next 7dc, "Dec A", 1dc in next dc, "Dec A", 1dc in each of next 7dc.
17dc.
9th Row: 1ch, 1dc in each of next 4dc, ("Dec B") 3 times, 1dc in each of next 4dc.
11dc.
10th Row: As 6th row.
Using grey, work 11 rows.
Fasten off.
Using a flat seam, join sole and leg seam, filling as you go and leaving top open. Sew legs to body.

TAIL:
Using 3.50mm hook and 2 strands of grey tog, make 25ch.
Fasten off.
Sew tail in position. Using red, tie a bow to end of tail.

PINAFORE DRESS (beg at top):
Using 3.50mm hook and yellow, make 6ch.
1st Row: (right side): Miss 1ch, 1dc in each ch to end.
5dc.
2nd Row: 1ch, 1dc in each dc to end.
Rep 2nd row twice.
5th Row: 1ch, 1dc in each dc to end, DO NOT TURN, remove hook from work.
Join a small length of yellow to beg of same row, make 14ch. Fasten off.
Return to main work, make 15ch, turn.
6th Row: Miss 1ch, 1dc in each st to end.
33dc.
Using green, **7th Row:** (1dc, 1ch) in first dc, 2tr in next dc, * 1tr in each of next 2dc, 2tr in next dc, rep from * to last dc, 1tr in last dc.
44tr, counting turning ch as 1tr.
8th Row: (1dc, 1ch) in first tr, 1tr in each tr to end, 1tr in top of turning ch.
9th Row: (1dc, 1ch) in first tr, 2tr in next tr, * 1tr in each of next 3tr, 2tr in next tr, rep from * to last 2 sts, 1tr in next tr, 1tr in top of turning ch.
55tr.
Rep 8th row 3 times.
Fasten off.
Using a flat seam, join centre back seam.

STRAPS (make 2):
Using 3.50mm hook and green, make 16ch.
1st Row: Miss 1ch, 1dc in each ch to end.
15dc.
Fasten off.
Sew straps in position crossing over at back.

GIRL MOUSE WITH WHITE JUMPER

BODY, HEAD, ARMS, EARS, LEGS AND TAIL
Work as for Mouse with Pink Jumper, using white in place of pink for body and arms, and red in place of green for shoes.

PINAFORE DRESS
Work as for Mouse with Pink Jumper, working in stripes of 9 rows red, 1 row each yellow, green and red. Make straps, using red in place of green.

BOY MOUSE

BODY, HEAD, ARMS, EARS, LEGS AND TAIL
Work as for Mouse with Pink Jumper, using yellow in place of pink for body and arms, and yellow in place of green for shoes. Omit bow from tail.

PANTS (beg at lower edge).
Using 3.50mm hook and green, make 20ch.
1st Row: Miss 3ch, 1tr in each ch to end.
18tr, counting turning ch as 1tr.
2nd Row: (1dc, 1ch) in first tr, 1tr in each tr to end.
Rep 2nd row 5 times.
8th Row: Sl st across first 3 sts, (1dc, 1ch) in next tr, 1tr in each tr to last 2tr and turning ch, turn.
Cont on these 12 sts.
Rep 2nd row 4 times.
Fasten off.
Make another piece the same.
Using a flat seam, join leg and crotch seams, leaving an opening to thread tail through. Using 2 strands of green tog, make 24ch. Fasten off.
Make another length of chain the same. Sew lengths of chain to pants, crossing over at back.
Using brown, make 2 small bows and attach to shoes for laces.

MOTHER MOUSE

BODY, HEAD, ARMS, EARS, LEGS AND TAIL
Using 4mm hook in place of 3.50mm hook, work as for Mouse with Pink Jumper using yellow in place of pink for body and arms, and red in place of green for shoes. Omit bow on tail.

SKIRT (beg at top):
Using 4mm hook and blue, make 34ch.
1st Row: Miss 1ch, 1dc in each ch to end.
33dc.
Work rows 7 to 9 inclusive of pinafore dress once, then 8th row once.

Using yellow, **6th Row:** (1dc, 1ch) in first tr, * miss 1tr, (1tr, 1ch, 1tr) in next tr, rep from * to last tr and turning ch, miss 1tr, 1tr in top of turning ch.
Using red, **7th Row:** (1dc, 1ch) in first tr, (1tr, 1ch, 1tr) in each ch sp to end, 1tr in top of turning ch.
Rep 7th row 3 times, in stripes of 1 row each blue, yellow and red.
Using blue, **11th Row:** (1dc, 1ch) in first tr, * 1tr in next tr, 1tr in ch sp, 1tr in next tr, rep from * to end, 1tr in top of turning ch.
12th Row: 1ch, 1dc in each tr to end, 1dc in top of turning ch.
Fasten off.
Using a flat seam, join centre back seam. Using 2 strands of blue tog, make 56ch. Fasten off. Thread length of chain through 2nd row and tie as illustrated.

FATHER MOUSE

BODY, HEAD, ARMS, EARS, LEGS AND TAIL
Using 4mm hook in place of 3.50mm hook, work as for Mouse with Pink Jumper using white in place of pink for body and arms. Work 4 rows white and 6 rows brown in place of green for shoes. Omit bow on tail.

PANTS
Using 4mm hook, work as for pants of boy mouse.
Using white, embroider buttons on front of pants as pictured.
Using white, embroider laces on shoes as pictured, tying ends in a bow.

BOW TIE
Using 4mm hook and red, make 8ch.
1st Row: Miss 1ch, 1dc in each ch to end.
2nd Row: 1ch, 1dc in each dc to end.
Rep 2nd row twice.
Fasten off.
Catch centre of bow tie as illustrated and sew in position.

Boxes by Jillian Morrow

TRIANGULAR BOX △

Heavy white cardboard
40cm white fabric
Polyester wadding
1.5m black cord
1 black button
Craft glue
Adhesive tape

Using the diagram at right, draw the shape onto cardboard and cut out. Score along broken lines. Cut a piece of fabric for covering, adding a 1.5cm allowance all around. Cut a triangle of wadding for the box top and glue in position.

Cover the box with fabric (on scored side) using glue to hold fabric in position. Avoid pulling fabric tightly. Clip fabric at corners. Fold along scored lines and tape walls into position. Use tape to reinforce fold lines.

Cut fabric for lining adding 1.5cm allowance all around. Cut a wadding triangle for the inside base and glue into position.

Glue lining fabric inside box, turning under allowance and holding with glue.

Sew button onto lid centre. Stitch cord to box edges as shown leaving a loop at the front point of box long enough to reach the button.

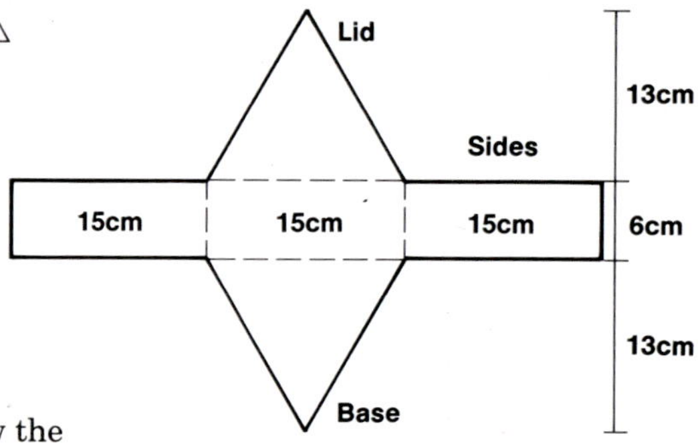

ROUND BOX △

Heavy white cardboard
40cm white fabric
Polyester wadding
1.5m black cord
1 black button
Craft glue
Adhesive tape

Use a bread and butter plate to draw two circles onto cardboard. Cut out these circles and measure the circumference for length of side panels. The measurement from the circles will be the length of the box wall (base and lid), allow an extra 1cm, which can be trimmed to fit when folded around. Make the width of the base wall 6cm and the width of the lid wall 2cm. Cut an extra box wall (insert) 7cm wide so that it will fit inside lid when finished.

Glue wadding to lid top and inside base to cover. Cut a circle of fabric to cover lid and base adding 1.5cm allowance. Cover lid, avoid pulling fabric tight, clip and glue allowance to wrong side. Stitch black button into centre of lid.

If desired, the base can be quilted by stitching fabric and wadding together at intervals before gluing. Using lid or base circle as a guide cut two extra circles of fabric without allowance. Glue these to the under-sides of lid and base to cover the turned fabric edges.

Cover box wall and insert wall with fabric, fold and glue neatly in place. For lid wall, join ends together and tape to form a circle then cover with fabric.

Join ends of insert wall (covered side in) together to form a circle and tape. Glue box wall with covered side out, around outside of insert wall circle leaving 2mm at the bottom to insert base.

Use pegs to secure sides while drying. Glue base into box wall fitting it in the 2mm space provided.

Glue lid to lid wall; trim box and lid with black cord, stitching in place.

Basket by students of Dover Heights College of TAFE (Commercial Needlecraft)

Shoe stuffers by Susan Massey

◁ SHOE STUFFERS

20cm x 90cm fabric
Polyester fibre fill
Lace
Ribbon

Enlarge diagram below using method shown on page 126. Cut four uppers and two soles.

With right sides together, pin and sew the three sections (two uppers and one sole) of each foot leaving back open. Turn out and stuff with fibre fill. Close openings by turning edge under then gather and stitch closed. Trim with lace and ribbon.

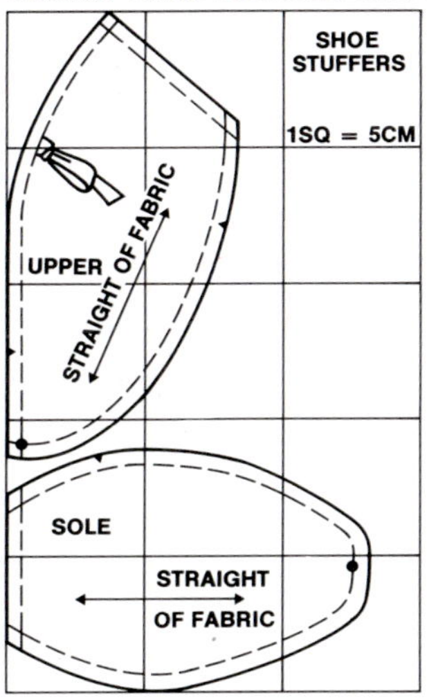

LINED BASKET △

Follow instructions for Lined Baskets on page 33.

INITIALLED HANDKERCHIEFS ▷

Purchased handkerchief
Stranded embroidery thread

Shadow work handkerchief (pictured overpage). Using diagram on page 89, enlarge to size desired and work letter on one corner of handkerchief in colours of your choice, using a single strand of thread.

If desired, work padded satin stitch flowers (below) near letter. See page 126 for explanation of stitches.

Cross stitch handkerchief (pictured on page 91). Work cross stitch designs using two strands embroidery thread following graph on page 90.

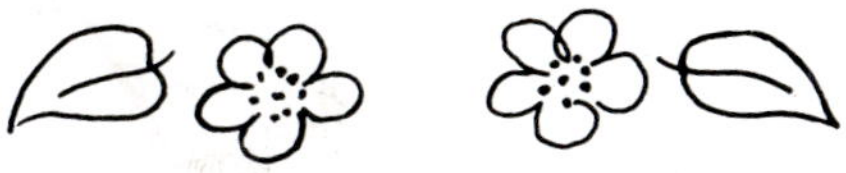

Initialled handkerchiefs by Christine Woodhead; crocheted edge handkerchiefs by Rosa Alonso

CROCHETED EDGE HANDKERCHIEFS △

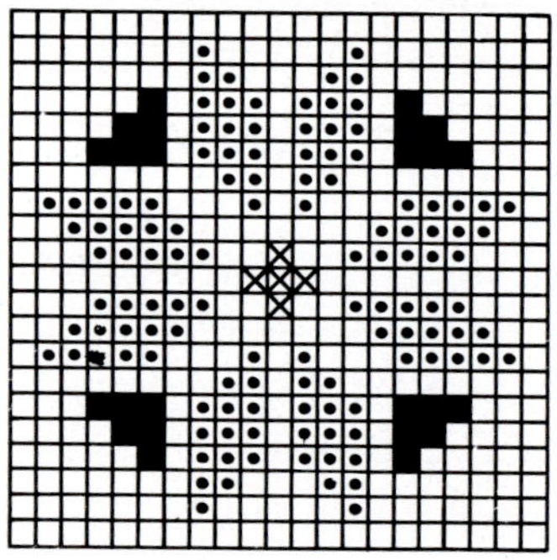

YARN REQUIREMENTS:
Crochet Cotton No. 20

For 3 handkerchiefs	1 ball

Abbreviations: See page 125.
Additional abbreviation: Lp = loop.
Accessories: One 0.75mm (No. 2) crochet hook; 3 handkerchiefs.

YELLOW HANDKERCHIEF
With right side of handkerchief facing, beg at corner.
1st Round: * Insert hook under handkerchief hem, yoh and draw through, yoh and draw through lp on hook, 3ch, miss 3mm of handkerchief, rep from * until there are 56 lps of 3ch. End with last st at next corner, cont to work 56 lps of 3ch in this way on 3 other edges, ending with sl st to 1st st.
2nd Round: Sl st to centre of 1st loop, 1dc in same place as last sl st, * (3ch, 1dc in centre of next loop) twice, 8 tr in next lp, 1dc in next lp, rep from * on all edges but end with sl st in 1st dc instead of 1dc in lp.
3rd Round: Sl st in each ch of 1st lp, 1ch, 1dc in next dc, * 3ch, (1tr, 1ch) in each of next 8tr, 3ch, miss 1 lp, 1dc in next dc, rep from * on all edges, ending with 3ch and sl st to 1st dc. Fasten off.

BLUE HANDKERCHIEF
1st Round: As yellow handkerchief.
2nd Round: Sl st to centre ch of 1st lp, 3ch, 1tr in same place as 3ch, * 2ch, 2tr in centre ch of next lp, rep from * on all edges, ending with 2ch and sl st to top of 3ch.
3rd Round: 1ch, 1dc in space between 3ch and 1tr, * 5ch, 1dc between 2tr, rep from *, ending with 5ch and sl st to 1st dc. Fasten off.

PINK HANDKERCHIEF
1st Round: As yellow handkerchief.
2nd Round: Sl st to centre ch of 1st lp, 1ch, 1dc in same ch as last sl st, * 3ch, 3tr in centre ch of next lp, 3ch, 1dc in centre ch of next lp, rep from * to end, but working sl st to 1st dc instead of 1dc. Fasten off.

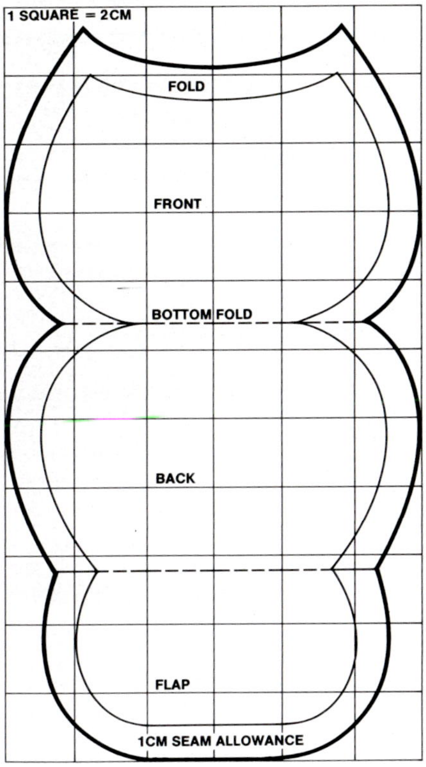

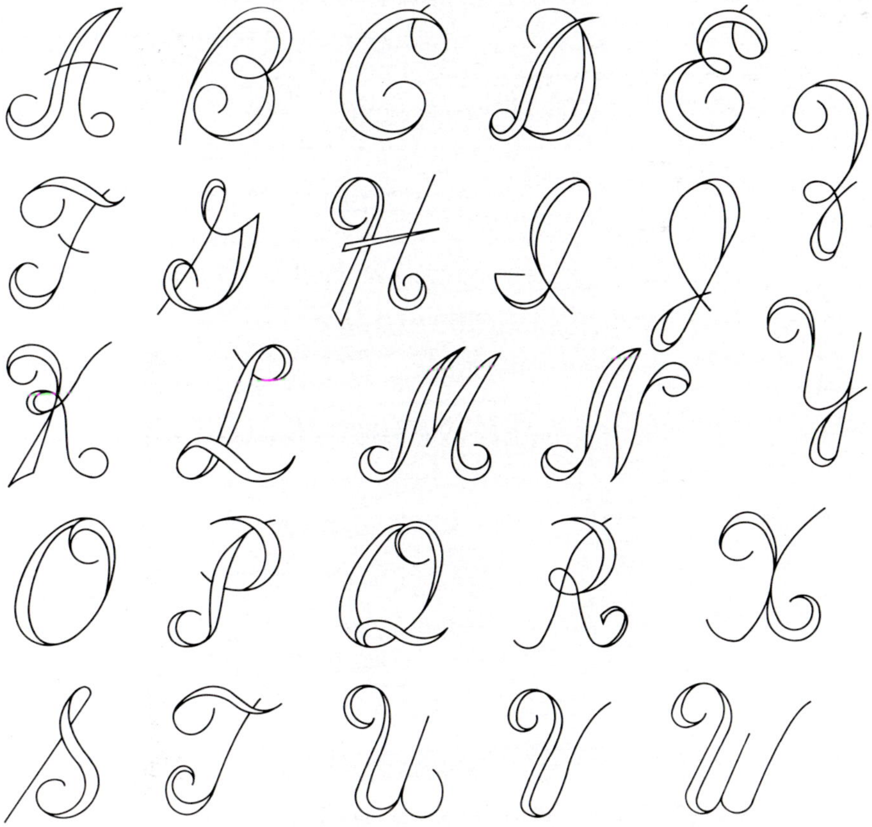

MONEY PURSE ▷

30cm x 20cm linen or Aida
Stranded embroidery thread
Snap fasteners
Scrap of lining fabric

Cut fabric and lining using pattern above. Enlarge chosen design and work on front of fabric in colours of your choice. Be sure to position design carefully. (Our star design was cross stitched on Aida fabric and the bow and initialled designs were done with shadow embroidery.)

Diagrams at left and above right. See page 126 for stitch instructions.

Turn in seam allowance on top of front section of fabric to face wrong side of fabric. Then fold up along bottom of purse with right sides facing. Repeat for lining.

Place lining on flat surface with the folded seam allowance facing upwards. Place fabric on top of lining with the seam allowance facing downwards and turn back and flap sections of fabric behind lining to encase it. Sew the fabric and lining together around side and flap seams. Leave bottom folded edges and folded seam edges unstitched. Turn inside out through opening. Press. Slip stitch folded seam allowances together. Attach snap fasteners.

Purses by Christine Woodhead

Necklaces by Christine Woodhead

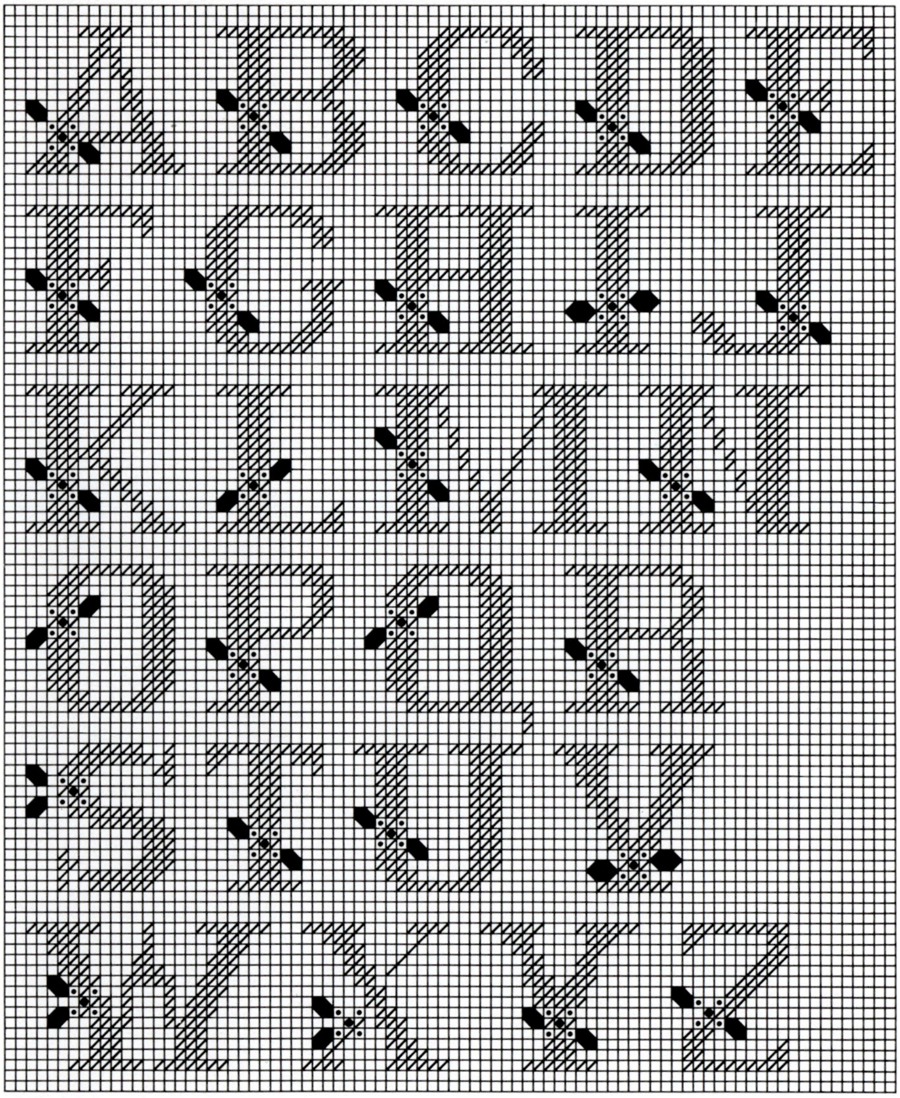

◁ NECKLACE

Small amounts linen, Aida or calico fabric
Stranded embroidery thread
Firm plastic
Ribbon or cord
Glue

Decide on size and shape of pendant then cut two pieces plastic and one piece wadding to desired size and shape (our finished rectangular pendant measures 4 x 4.5cm.

Cut fabric (6cm square) and, for cross stitch work the design using graph below, or use diagram on page 89 and work in running stitch outline and French knots. Use two strands of thread in colours of your choice. Press fabric with embroidery, face down on a terry towel cloth.

Trim fabric to 1cm larger than plastic. Cut backing fabric to match.

Glue wadding to plastic, then glue fabric with design onto wadding. Turn back 1cm over the plastic. Glue backing fabric to other piece plastic and turn back edges.

Glue front and back sections together. To make a cord twist a length of stranded thread, holding at both ends. Pick up the thread at the centre and allow it to twist around itself. Glue twisted cord around edges of pendant and make a loop to hang pendant.

Thread ribbon or cord through loop to hang pendant around neck.

INITIALLED POTPOURRI SACHET ▷

Sachet and handkerchief by Christine Woodhead

20cm Aida fabric
Stranded embroidery thread
30cm x 5cm lace
Ribbon
Potpourri

Cut two circles, 20cm diameter, from Aida fabric. Cross stitch desired letter, on one piece of fabric using graph at left and two strands of thread in colours of your choice. See page 126 for stitch instructions.

Gather straight edge of lace and stitch to right side of initialled fabric so fancy edge is facing inwards. Place Aida fabric pieces, right sides together and stitch, leaving a small opening at top. Turn through opening to right side. Fill with potpourri and stitch on a ribbon loop. Stitch opening closed.

GIRL'S COAT HANGER △

30cm wooden coat hanger
48cm x 16cm cotton fabric
Polyester wadding (thick)
50cm x 2cm-wide broderie lace
Ribbon

Remove hook from hanger. Cut piece of wadding length of hanger plus 1cm extra each end and 12cm wide. Fold in half lengthwise and stitch along long ends allowing 1cm seam. (This can be stitched by hand onto hanger, if desired.) Enclose ends of wadding and stitch in place if desired.

Pin lace to right side of one long edge with scalloped edge facing inwards. Baste.

Fold fabric in half lengthwise, right sides together and machine. Turn to right side and press.

Run gathering thread 15mm from both edges and pull in to required length to fit hanger. Pull evenly over hanger and enclose ends with hand stitching. Secure gathering by machine stitching twice over gathering stitches.

To cover hook cut 15cm bias strip. Fold right sides together and stitch. Pull through to right side. Screw hook into hole at top of hanger. Tie a bow with ribbon and secure in place with hand stitches.

Initialled handkerchief instructions on page 87.

INITIALLED BUTTON △

Aida fabric scrap
Stranded embroidery thread
Plastic
Glue
29mm self cover buttons
Safety pin

Mark outline of button on fabric. Centre and embroider desired letter using cross stitch from graph at left and two strands of thread in colours of your choice. Follow packet instructions to cover button.

To make a badge, cut a piece of plastic to cover back of button. Glue in place. Attach a safety pin with glue.

LINEN BOOKMARK ▽

22cm x 12cm piece of linen
Stranded embroidery thread

Work cross stitch letter 6.5cm from bottom of fabric in centre. Work from graph on page 90 in colours of your choice. Outline leaves using back stitch and work half cross stitch where necessary.

Measure 3cm from top of fabric, remove several horizontal threads, work hem stitch across the linen on the wrong side. Repeat at bottom of fabric. Press the embroidery face down on a bath towel with an iron. Fold under 2cm along the long edges of fabric, then fold again so the folded edges meet at centre back. Use slipstitch to join folded edges.

See page 126 for stitch instructions.

AIDA BAND BOOKMARK ▽

22cm Aida band
Stranded embroidery thread

Cut a piece of Aida band 22cm long.

Work the cross stitch letter from graph on page 90 using two strands of thread and colours of your choice. Use half cross stitch on leaves where necessary and outline in back stitch. Position the letter 6.5cm from bottom of band and in the centre of the band.

Measure 3cm from top of band, hem stitch across the band at this point. Repeat at bottom of band. Unravel top and bottom of band to hemline to form fringe.

See page 126 for stitch instructions.

Bookmarks by Christine Woodhead

Box by Neryl Hogan

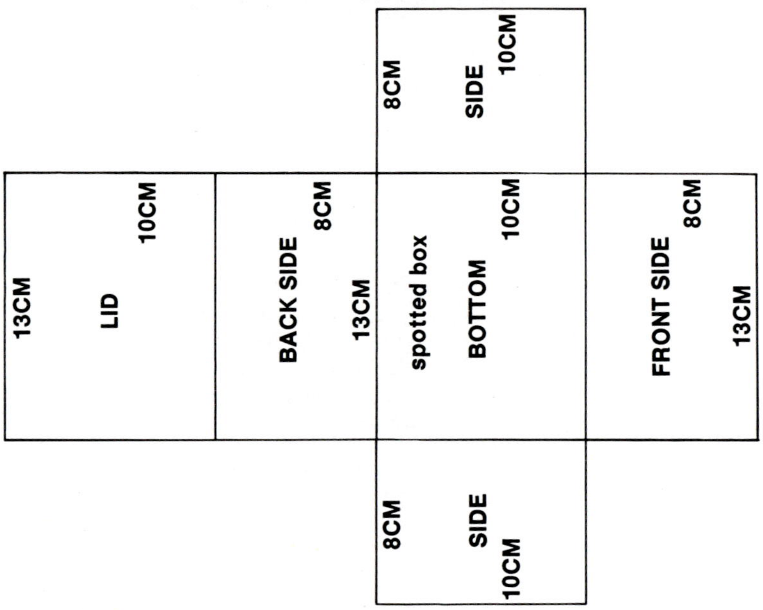

SPOTTED COVERED BOX △

Heavy cardboard
Thin wadding
50cm fabric
Sharp knife
Craft glue
Adhesive tape

Draw box onto cardboard from pattern at left. Cut extra rectangles of cardboard to line lid, sides, front side and back side.

Trim lining pieces slightly smaller so they fit inside the box. Cover all lining pieces with fabric using glue.

Score along lines of box with sharp knife making sure not to

GRANDMA'S FRAMES ▽

Light cardboard
Small amount fabric
Braid or lace
Small amount ribbon
Craft glue

Cut one piece cardboard 14cm x 6.5cm. Cut one piece cardboard 13cm x 6cm. Fold smaller piece in half. On each side, place a small photograph in centre and trace around it. Mark a line 5mm in from traced line, then cut out marked area for photograph hole.

Cover large piece cardboard with fabric by gluing it in place. Glue lace around edge, if desired and glue braid across fabric as desired.

Glue a 15cm piece ribbon half way down each narrow edge, this will form the tie to close the frame.

Cover smaller piece cardboard with fabric, cut out material from hole in centre; fold back and glue on underside. When covering this piece put glue in middle between cut-outs as well as around edges.

With wrong sides together, glue smaller piece cardboard to larger piece along top and bottom edges. Leave sides of smaller piece free to insert photographs.

cut through cardboard. Glue wadding to scored side of box and cover with fabric.

Fold box into shape and glue along edges to secure. Use tape at edges for extra strength.

Decorate with braid as desired and make a loop at the front to lift lid. Glue lining pieces in position.

Frames by Neryl Hogan

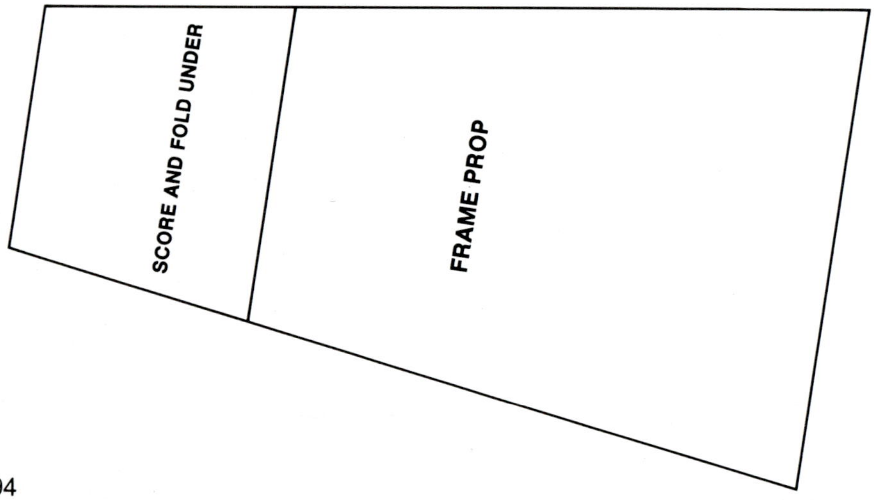

△ FLORAL FRAME

Heavy cardboard
50cm cotton fabric
Wadding
Craft glue
Ribbon
Braid

Make in the same way as the Satin Photograph Frame. The measurements for our frame were 23cm x 19.5cm for large pieces and 18cm x 14.5cm for small piece.

◁ THREE-IN-ONE OVAL PICTURE FRAME

Heavy cardboard
70cm cotton fabric
Wadding
Braid
Craft glue
Ribbon

Cut three pieces cardboard in desired shape for frame. Our frame was 44cm x 11.5cm with curved ends.

On one piece cardboard mark position of photographs and cut oval holes. Cover one side with wadding, cut wadding away from holes then cover with fabric, gluing edges to wrong side. Glue braid around photograph holes.

For backing piece, glue wadding to one piece cardboard, cover with fabric. Snip fabric at curves to allow for flat finish.

For middle layer, cover remaining piece cardboard with fabric only. If hanging by ribbon loop, glue loop to this covered piece. Glue backing and middle pieces together with wrong sides facing.

Glue remaining front frame piece to backing section around top, bottom and one side, leaving one side open to insert photographs. Glue braid around edges.

Decorate with ribbon roses, if desired (see page 126 for rose instructions).

Frames by Keryl Egan

◁ SATIN PHOTOGRAPH FRAME

Heavy cardboard
50cm satin fabric
Wadding
Craft glue
Ribbon
Brass corners

Cut two pieces cardboard 32cm x 28cm. Cut one piece cardboard 27cm x 20cm. (The small piece of cardboard forms the frame around the picture.) Cut hole in smaller piece cardboard 1cm smaller than photograph. Glue wadding to one side of this piece cardboard, then cover with fabric. Snip fabric at corners to allow for flat finish.

To cut fabric away from photograph hole snip in the centre of the hole, cut a square smaller than hole, cut at each corner and glue to underside.

Glue wadding to one large piece cardboard then cover with fabric. Cover other large piece cardboard with fabric only. Glue large pieces together, wrong sides facing. Be careful using glue on satin fabric as it can stain.

Glue frame piece to large padded piece along top, bottom and one side, leaving the other side free to insert photograph.

To make frame prop cut two pieces cardboard using pattern at left. Score and cover both pieces with fabric and glue together so that the scoring is on the outside of both pieces.

Turn back the scored square on the prop. Glue one end of a piece of ribbon on the prop stand and the other end to scored square section to hold the prop in place. Glue square area of prop onto the back of frame.

The frame can also be hung by attaching a loop to the back and near the top of the frame.

Slip brass corners on to frame. Glue in place.

PINK CAT BOX ▽

Medium size, sturdy fruit box
2m cotton fabric
Polyester wadding
Craft glue
1.5m thin cord
Polyester fibre fill

Cut any flaps off top of box and cut a wide-bottom 'V' shape into one of the long sides. Glue wadding to inside sides and back of box then cover box with fabric and glue in place. (Pegs will help hold fabric in place while glue is drying.)

Measure inside area of box for the cushion and cut out from remaining fabric adding 3cm all around for wadding and joins.

To make up cushion sew fabric together with wrong sides out, leaving 10cm for wadding. Turn out, fill so cushion is about 3cm thick and sew gap.

Put a few hand stitches in cushion to give a quilted effect. Lastly stitch or glue cord around outside edge to finish.

Box by Jillian Morrow

Combs by Gabriella Verstraeten

◁RIBBON ROSE HAIR COMBS

Bunches of ribbon roses (white or yellow roses take colours best)
Hair combs
Fine paint brush
Fabric dyes

Wrap flowers around the top of a hair comb, twisting wire ends of flowers together to secure them.

Using fabric dyes, dab colours onto roses with a fine paint brush. It is usually best to select green for the flower base to ensure none of the original colour shows through.

Allow dyes to dry thoroughly before wearing.

BRAID AND LACE HAIR COMBS▷

Small amount braid or lace
Small amount ribbon
Dried or ribbon flowers
Craft glue

To make lace covered comb, cut piece of lace slightly longer than comb, then glue in place turning ends under. Decorate with flowers if desired.

To make braid covered comb glue end of braid to back of comb, then weave between first tooth and over top, continuing until all covered.

Cover end of braid as you work. Glue other end of braid to back of comb. Decorate with bows or ribbon if desired.

▽ RIBBON HAIR COMBS

2 hair combs
Small amount cotton fabric
50cm x 3mm ribbon
Craft glue

Measure fabric over the top edge of hair comb and double the amount. A double amount makes it easier to sew and covers better. Cut out measured amount, fold the outside long edges in towards the centre and fold over comb with folded edges underneath.

Stitch (or glue) fabric, sewing through the teeth of the comb. Tie a small bow with the ribbon, position and glue, trim ends.

Braid and lace combs by Neryl Hogan; ribbon combs by Jillian Morrow

Shoes by Rosa Alonso

BRAID TRIM SHOES △

1 pair happy shoes
1m braid

Pin braid to happy shoes in desired design. Stitch around edges of braid with invisible stitches to secure it to shoes.

Ukata shave coat by Weiss Pringle

TERRACOTTA POTS ▷

Terracotta pot and saucer
Vinyl or acrylic paints
Paint brush

Trace design from patterns on page 98 and 99 onto rim of pot or saucer, with pencil. Paint design in desired colour and allow to dry.

Pots pictured overpage.

Pots painted by Sue Cadzow

Box by Jillian Morrow

RECTANGULAR BOX △

Heavy cardboard
40cm fabric
Polyester wadding
Craft glue
Adhesive tape

Use diagram at right to cut out box in cardboard, cut two each of the side panel inserts.

Score cardboard along broken lines using a sharp knife. Glue a wadding rectangle to top of lid only.

Cut fabric to cover each piece, adding 2cm allowance. Cover scored side of box, lid and also side panel inserts with fabric using glue and turning allowances to wrong side. Fold up box and lid; use glue and tape to hold sides in position. Cut two extra pieces of fabric, 10cm x 15cm, and glue to inside lid and on bottom of base to cover turned edges. Glue side panel inserts in place.

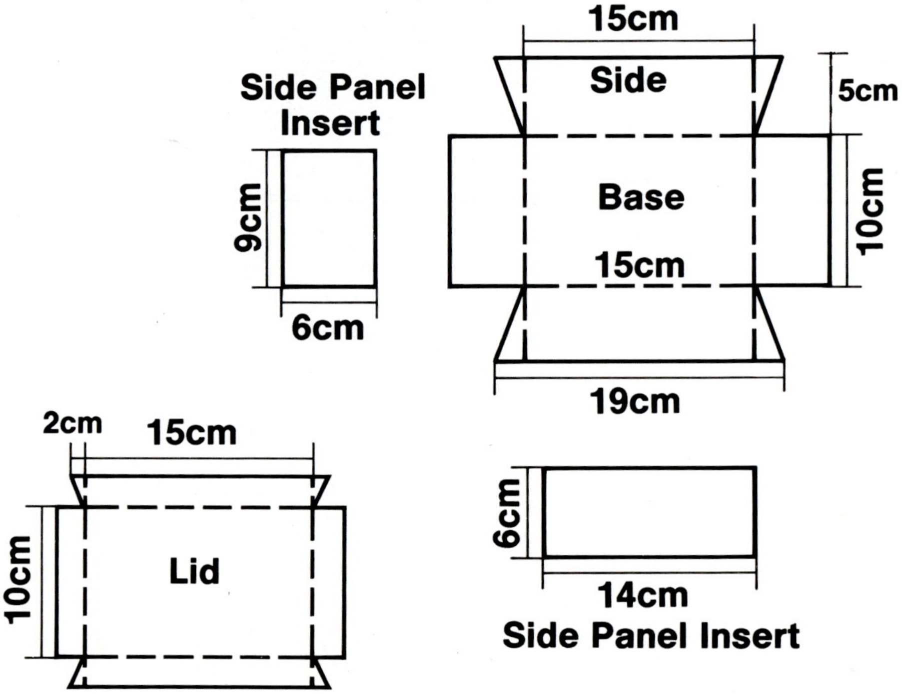

COVERED WRITING COMPENDIUM ▷

Heavy cardboard
2m lace
60cm fabric
Craft glue
Thin wadding

Cut one piece cardboard 44cm x 27cm for writing compendium. Cut another piece slightly smaller. Score two lines across centre 27cm width to form spine.

Cut two pieces cardboard 27cm x 8cm for inside flaps.

Cut piece of wadding same size as compendium and glue to outside. Cut fabric 1.5cm larger than compendium. Cover, turning 1.5cm allowance to inside, and gluing in place.

Cover smaller compendium lining with wadding then fabric. Glue lace around edge. Glue outside and inside pieces together.

Cut two pieces wadding same size as flaps and glue in place, then cover flaps with fabric. Glue lace to inside long edge of flaps. Glue flaps to inside ends of compendium so wadding side is facing outwards. Make sure flaps are free of glue on the long lace edged side nearest the spine.

Compendium by Neryl Hogan

Books covered by Neryl Hogan

◁COVERED ADDRESS BOOKS

Address books
20cm fabric (varies)
Light cardboard
Wadding
1m braid
1m lace (if desired)
Craft glue

To make soft covered notebook, cut two pieces cardboard slightly smaller than book covers. Cover with fabric by gluing in place.

Cut piece of wadding same size as outside cover and glue in place.

Cut piece fabric 1cm larger than outside cover and glue over wadding turning allowance to inside. Apply lace to inside edge if desired. Glue braid in place. Glue inside covers in place. Glue braid around edges of book.

Note. Some notebooks have a hard cover which can be padded and covered. Use inside pages as inside covers; simply glue pages down instead of covering cardboard inner covers.

EMBROIDERED CARDS

Cartridge paper
Spray adhesive
Scraps of silk organza
Beads
Fusible webbing (paper backed and double sided)
Coloured foil or paper

Cut paper to size desired for card and fold in half. Spray one half (the front) with spray adhesive.

Lay a piece of organza over the front half of card, trim to edges. Iron double sided webbing to the wrong side of selected fabrics for leaf, flowers and centres. Cut out the desired shapes, peel off paper and iron on to card.

Applique (zigzag machine stitch) flowers and leaves down to secure in place.

Stitch around outside edge of card to frame it. Trim threads and edges then hand stitch the beads in place as desired.

To make foil card, place pieces of foil under organza. Finish with beads and stitch around edges as above.

RIBBON TRIMMED STATIONERY

Sheet of writing paper (medium to heavy weight)
Matching envelopes
Ribbon

Gently undo the envelope so that it is flat. Using a variety of left over pieces of ribbon, glue the ribbon down in desired design by applying small dots of glue.

Wait until glue is dry before proceeding. Stitch through the ribbon using machine straight or zigzag stitch. Trim threads and ribbon. Glue up envelope.

To decorate writing paper glue ribbon and stitch in place as for envelope.

Stationery on this page by Gabriella Verstraeten

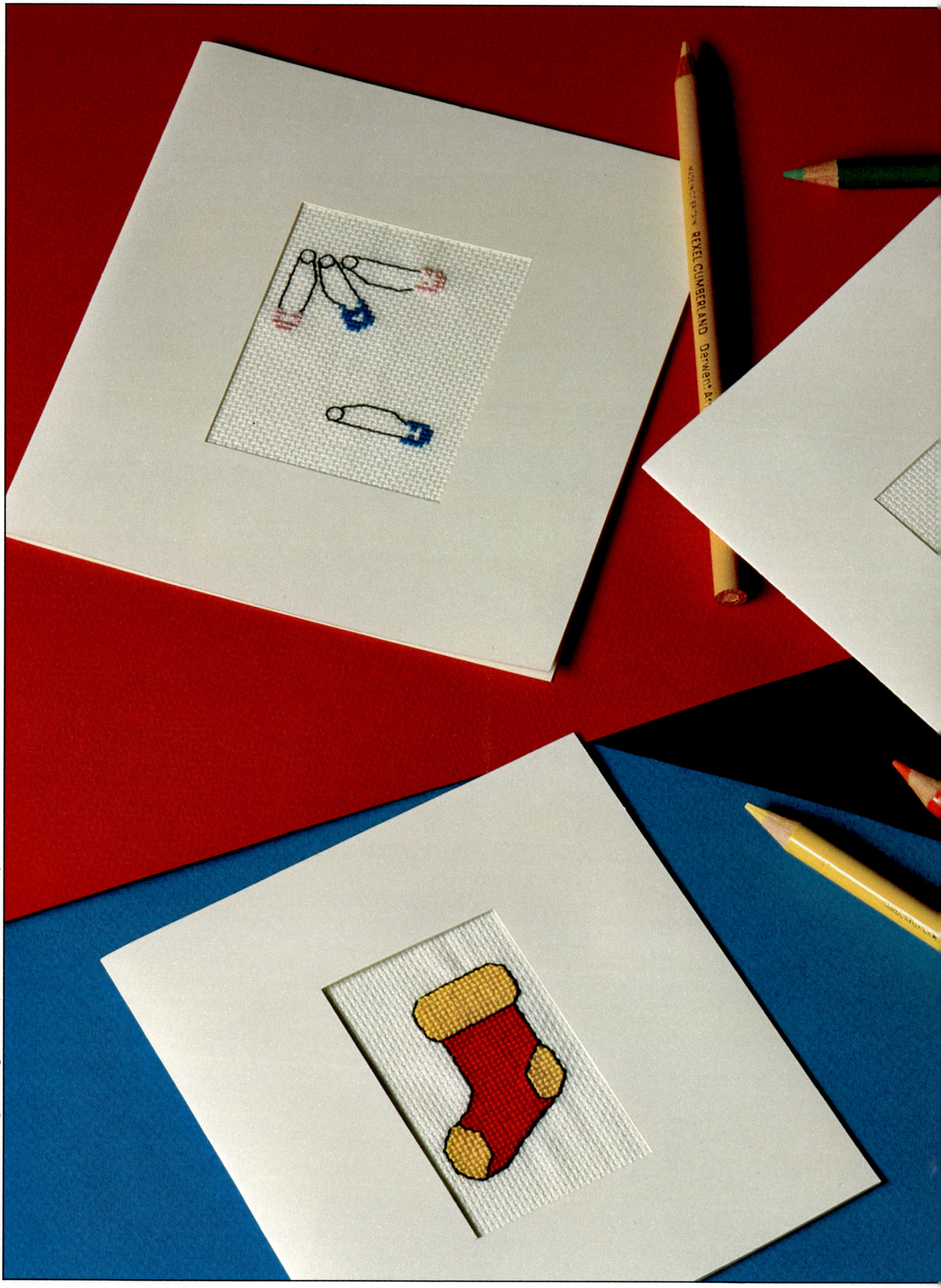

Cards by students of Dover Heights College of TAFE (Commercial Needlecraft)

◁ CROSS STITCH CARDS

Heavyweight paper
Scrap of Aida fabric
Stranded embroidery thread (refer to key on graph for thread colours)
Glue

Work design on Aida fabric following graph below and using two strands of thread (see page 126 for cross stitch). Allow 2cm around all edges of design.

Cut paper to desired size for card and fold in half. Cut out a square in centre front of card slightly larger than design. Glue cross stitched fabric to inside of front of card so it is showing through the hole.

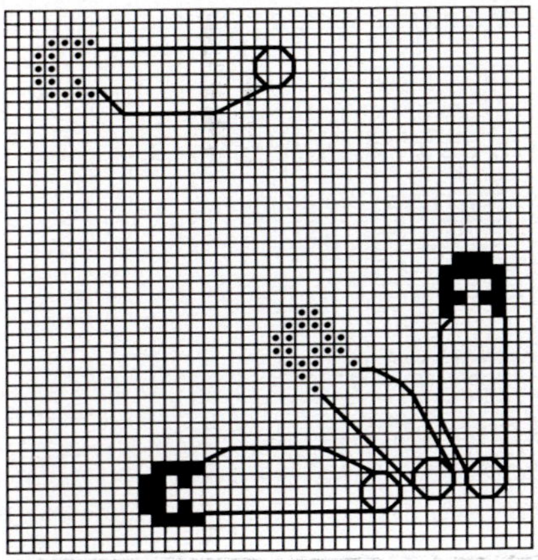

■ DMC 3689
⊡ DMC 995
— DMC 310

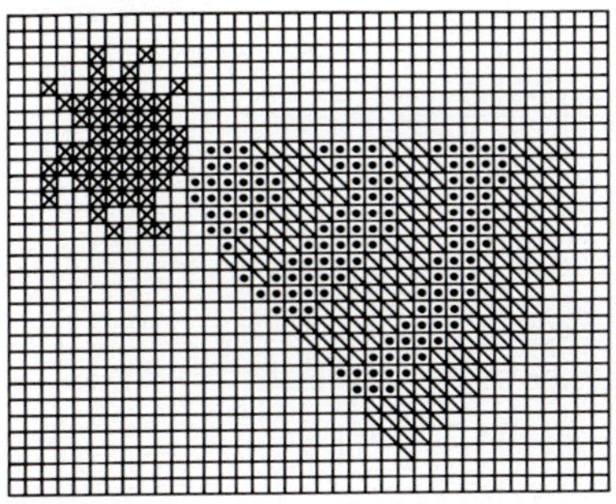

☒ DMC 973
⊡ DMC 995
◪ DMC 608

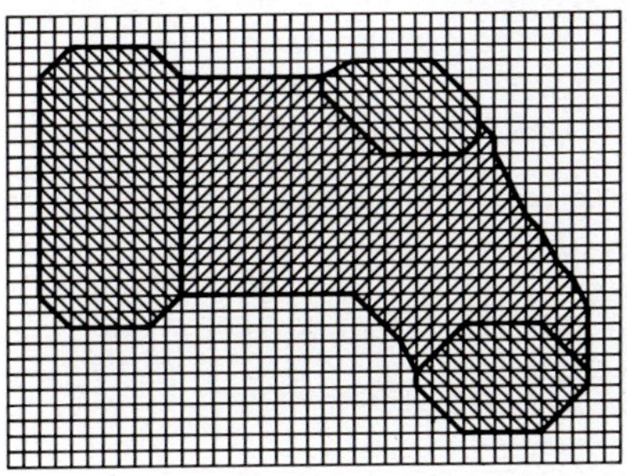

◪ DMC 973
⧅ DMC 666
— DMC 310

BRIDAL COAT HANGER ▷

40cm wooden coat hanger
64cm x 20cm satin fabric
Polyester wadding (3cm thick)
1m x 4cm-wide lace edging
20cm satin bias binding

Remove coat hanger hook. Cut piece of wadding length of hanger plus 1cm extra each end and 12cm wide. Fold in half lengthwise and stitch along long edges with 1cm seam allowed. (This can be stitched by hand on to hanger or by machine and then slipped over hanger). Enclose ends of wadding and stitch in place.

Pin lace edging to right side of one long edge of fabric with scalloped edge facing inwards. Baste, fold fabric in half, right sides together and machine.

Turn to right side and press. Run gathering threads 15mm from top and 10mm from bottom edge. Pull up gathering so fabric is same length as hanger. Check fabric is evenly gathered over hanger. Secure gathering by machine stitching twice over gathering stitches. Enclose ends by hand stitching.

To cover hook cut 20cm length of satin binding, fold right-sides together and stitch. Pull through to right side. Slip over hook and secure at end with hand stitching. Screw hook into hole at top of hanger, making a small cut in the fabric and securing this raw edge with hand stitching. Form roses from lace by folding lace over width wise, about four times and stitch at base to secure. Make two roses, tie ribbon to secure roses together and stitch in place on hanger.

BRIDAL GARTER ▷

1.4m x 23mm-wide satin ribbon
40cm x 5mm-wide elastic
2.8m ungathered lace
10cm narrow ribbon
Fabric flowers
Craft glue

Cut ribbon into two 70cm pieces. Lay wrong sides together with lace in between. Stitch 5mm from each edge of ribbon, stitching in lace.

Thread elastic through centre casing and stitch along centre, stretching elastic as you sew. Join ends and decorate with fabric flowers and a ribbon bow.

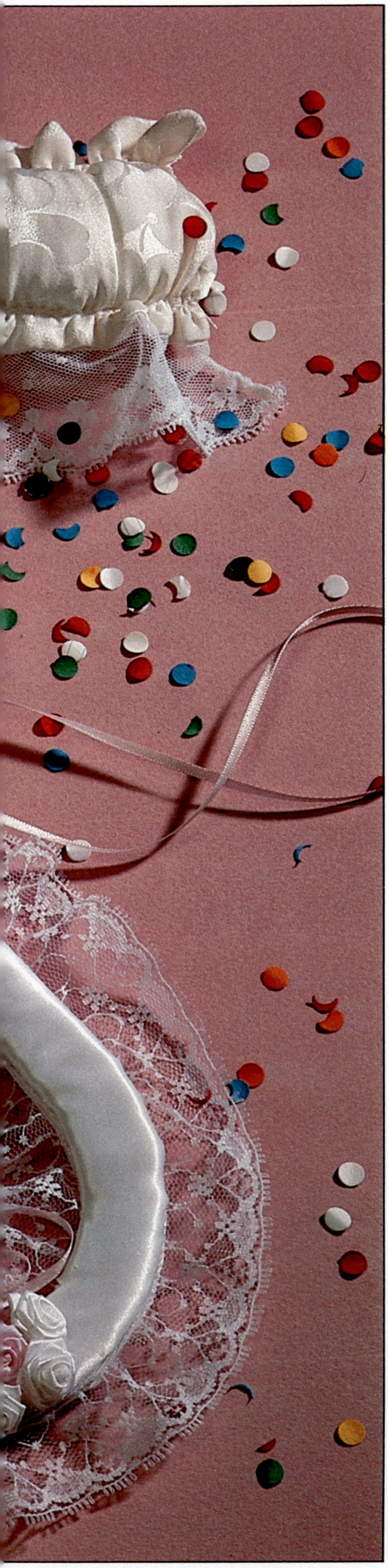

Handkerchief by Rosa Alonso; garter and horseshoe by Neryl Hogan; hanger by Joan Danaher

◁WHITE HANDKERCHIEF WITH TATTED EDGING

YARN REQUIREMENTS:

Crochet cotton No. 20	1 ball

Accessories: Tatting shuttle; linen handkerchief.

Abbreviations: R (ring): Closing. When the loops are formed into stitches, slide them in turn along the circle of thread and hold them in position between the thumb and forefinger.

Ds (double stitches): With the thread in position, drop the middle finger of the left hand and move the shuttle forward and insert it under both threads of left hand and bring it back over the circle of thread held between the thumb and the forefinger of the left hand and under the shuttle thread. Drop the thread from the little finger of the right hand and draw the shuttle thread taut with a sharp jerk relaxing the fingers of the left hand. Slowly raise the middle finger on the left hand sliding the loop into position between the thumb and forefinger.

P (picot): Draw the first half of the double stitch to within a little space from previous one instead of close to it. Work a second half of double stitch.

EDGING: R (ring) of 4ds (double stitches) 3ps (picots) separated by 5ds, 4ds, close. * space, r of 4ds, 3ps separated by 5ds, 4ds, close; repeat from *.

TO MAKE UP:
Sew to handkerchief.

◁BRIDAL HORSE SHOE

Satin fabric
Wadding
Heavy cardboard
Lace
Ribbon
Fabric flowers
Glue

Draw horse shoe shapes onto cardboard and cut two pieces. Cover both sides with wadding by gluing it in place.

Cover with fabric, snipping around curved edges. Glue lace trim to wrong side of one piece.

Make a loop of ribbon and attach to wrong side of one piece.

Glue pieces together, wrong sides facing. Trim with flowers and ribbon as desired.

WEDDING PHOTOGRAPH ALBUM▷

Photograph album
1m cotton fabric (amount varies)
Heavy cardboard
2m lace
1m ribbon
Wadding
Craft glue
Spray adhesive

Cut wadding to size of photograph album and glue to covers using spray adhesive. Cover with fabric using spray adhesive as you would a book, using mitred corners and push pieces at the centre top and bottom into the spine.

Cut two pieces cardboard 5mm smaller than covers. (These form the inside covers). Cover with same fabric as album cover or use contrasting fabric, if desired.

Glue lace around edges on wrong side of lining pieces. Glue a piece of ribbon halfway down each edge of lining pieces for ties. Glue lining pieces to inside covers of album.

Cut a piece of cardboard smaller than album page. (Our frame was 18.5cm x 14.5cm). Cut hole for photograph in centre.

Glue wadding to cardboard and cover with fabric. Trim with lace by gluing it to wrong side, if desired.

Trim with ribbon roses if desired (see page 126 for instructions).

WEDDING CHARMS ▷

YARN REQUIREMENTS:
Patons Gem 4 Ply (50g) Balls

Abbreviations: See page 125. Additional abbreviations below.
Accessories: 1 set 3.25mm (No. 10) knitting needles for Parasol, 3mm (No. 10-11) crochet hook for Horseshoe; pipe cleaner and fabric stiffener for Parasol; cardboard for Horseshoe; ribbon.
Additional Abbreviations: "M2" = (K1, P1) into front of next st.
"M3" = (K1, P1, K1) into front of next st.
"Picot" = 4ch, sl st in 4th ch from hook.

PARASOL (beg at centre)
Cast on 8 sts (3, 3, 2). Join into a round, taking care not to twist cast-on edge.
1st Round: Knit.
2nd Round: *Y fwd, K1, rep from * to end.
16 sts.
Knit 3 rounds.
6th Round: As 2nd round.
32 sts.
Knit 3 rounds.
10th Round: K1, * y fwd, K2, rep from * to last st, y fwd, K1.
48 sts.
11th Round: K1, * "M2", K2, rep from * to last 2 sts, "M2", K1.
64 sts.
12th Round: * K2 tog, y fwd, sl 1, K1, psso, rep from * to end.
48 sts.
Rep 11th and 12th rounds 4 times.
21st Round: K1, * "M3", K2, rep from * to last 2 sts, "M3", K1.
80 sts.
Knit 3 rounds.
25th Round: * Y fwd, K5, rep from * to end.
96 sts.
26th and Alt Rounds: Knit.
27th Round: * K1, y fwd, sl 1, K1, psso, K1, K2 tog, y fwd, rep from * to end.
29th Round: * Y fwd, K2 tog, y fwd, sl 1, K2 tog, psso, y fwd, K1, rep from * to end.
31st Round: * Sl 1, K1, psso, y fwd, rep from * to end.
33rd Round: * Y fwd, K2 tog, rep from * to end.
34th Round: Knit.
35th Round: Knit first st, * slip st from right-hand needle back on to left-hand needle, insert needle into this st and cast on 2 sts, then cast off 5 sts, rep from * until all sts have been cast off.

TO MAKE UP:
With a slightly damp cloth and warm iron, press lightly. Stiffen with fabric stiffener. Place pipe cleaner through centre ring for 1cm and catch in position. Catch top edge to pipe cleaner at 6 even intervals. Bend pipe cleaner at top to form handle. Cut a piece of ribbon 60cm long and fold to make a loop, attach to handle together with a small bow as illustrated.

HORSESHOE
1ST PIECE
Make 40ch.
1st Row: Miss 1ch, 1dc in each of next 13ch, (2dc in next ch, 1dc in next ch) 6 times, 2dc in next ch, 1dc in each of last 13ch.
2nd and Alt Rows: 1ch, 1dc in each dc to end.
3rd Row: 1ch, 1dc in each of first 14dc, (2dc in next dc, 1dc in each of next 2dc) 6 times, 2dc in next dc, 1dc in each of last 13dc.
5th Row: 1ch, 1dc in each of first 14dc, (2dc in next dc, 1dc in each of next 3dc) 6 times, 2dc in next dc, 1dc in each of last 14dc.
7th Row: 1ch, 1dc in each of first 15dc, (2dc in next dc, 1dc in each of next 4dc) 6 times, 2dc in next dc, 1dc in each of last 14dc.
Work 1 round of dc evenly around entire horseshoe, having a number of dc divisible by 4. **
Next Round: 1ch, * 1dc in each of next 4dc, "Picot", rep from * to end, join with a sl st.
Fasten off.
2ND PIECE
Work as for 1st Piece to **
Fasten off.

TO MAKE UP:
Cut a piece of cardboard the same size as 2nd Piece. Place 2 pieces tog with cardboard between and sew 2nd Piece to 1st Piece at base of Picot row. Cut a length of ribbon 50cm long, fold in half and sew to top of horseshoe. Make a small bow and sew to front as illustrated.

Album by Neryl Hogan

RIGHT: Wedding Charms and Wedding Photograph Album (album instructions on page 107).

Hanger by Neryl Hogan

△ COVERED COAT HANGER WITH POTPOURRI OPENING

Wire coat hanger
Heavy cardboard
Lace fabric
Potpourri
Craft glue
20cm x 115cm fabric
Braid
Dried flowers (if desired)
Wadding

Lay coat hanger on cardboard and trace around. Cut two pieces.

Cut an oval or circular shape in one piece. (This is for the lace potpourri section).

To make potpourri bag cut two pieces lace 3cm larger all around than the hole in the cardboard. Glue edges together, leaving one end open. Fill with potpourri and glue opening together.

Cover two pieces cardboard with wadding. Cut back the wadding over piece with hole. Cover pieces with fabric. Snip fabric covering piece with hole back to the cardboard edges at 5mm intervals. Glue fabric edges to back of cardboard.

If trimming with lace, glue around edges of front piece and around hole in front cover. Glue potpourri bag in place in hole.

While front and back pieces are drying cover coat hanger hook with braid or ribbon by coating one side of braid or ribbon with glue and winding it around hanger.

Spread glue around edges of front and back covers. Place hanger in position and join covers together over hanger. Hold together with pegs or sticky tape until dry.

If trimming with braid, glue around edges. Trim with bows and flowers, if desired.

CHRISTENING ROBE COAT HANGER ▷

30cm wooden hanger
44cm x 14cm lace edging
44cm x 14cm voile or lining tafetta
44cm x 10cm lace edging for bow
20cm satin bias binding
Polyester wadding (1cm thick)

Cut coat hanger down to 25cm. Cut piece of wadding, length of hanger plus 1cm extra each end. Fold in half lengthwise and stitch along long edges allowing 1cm seam. (This can be stitched by hand onto hanger.) Enclose ends of wadding and stitch in place. Hand baste lining to lace fabric.

Pin lace edging to right side of one long edge of fabric with scalloped or finished edge facing inwards then baste.

Fold fabric in half, right sides together and machine. Turn to right side and press.

Run gathering threads 12mm from both edges and pull up to length required to fit hanger. Pull evenly over hanger. Secure gathering by machining twice over gathering stitches. Enclose ends with hand stitching.

To cover hook cut 20cm length binding. Fold, right sides together and stitch along edge. Pull through to right side, slip over hook and secure end with hand stitching.

Screw hook into hole at top of coat hanger (back of work). Tie lace bow around hook.

Hanger by Joan Danaher

Hanger by Neryl Hogan

◁SHIRT COAT HANGER

Wire coat hanger
Heavy cardboard
20cm x 115cm fabric
Contrast fabric scrap
Lace
Ribbon
Braid
Craft glue
Wadding

Make hanger in the same way as Covered Coat Hanger with Potpourri Opening omitting potpourri and opening.

Glue ribbon and lace in place to resemble a shirt front. Cut contrast fabric scrap into shape to make a collar and pocket top. Press and glue raw edges under and glue onto the hanger.

LADY'S SHIRT BAG△

40cm cotton print fabric
10cm contrasting fabric
12 self cover buttons
40cm Velcro

Cut one piece fabric 37cm x 32cm and one piece 34cm x 32cm. Devise your own design for shirt, referring to picture.

Cut contrasting fabric for collar and band. Cover buttons following manufacturer's instructions. Applique contrast fabric onto bag using machine satin stitch. Sew buttons onto band section.

Make Velcro opening along 32cm edge as for lingerie bag. Finish as for lingerie bag on page 114.

MAN'S SHIRT BAG▷

40cm cotton fabric
10cm contrast fabric
2 buttons
40cm Velcro

Cut one piece fabric 35cm x 39cm and one piece fabric 35cm x 36cm, or desired size.

Devise your own design for shirt referring to picture. Cut tie from contrast fabric. Machine satin stitch design on larger piece fabric and applique tie. Stitch buttons in place.

Form Velcro opening along 35cm edge as for lingerie bag. Finish as for lingerie bag on page 114.

Travel bags by Rosa Alonso

LEFT: Lady's Shirt Bag. BELOW LEFT: Man's Shirt Bag. ABOVE: Lingerie Bag.

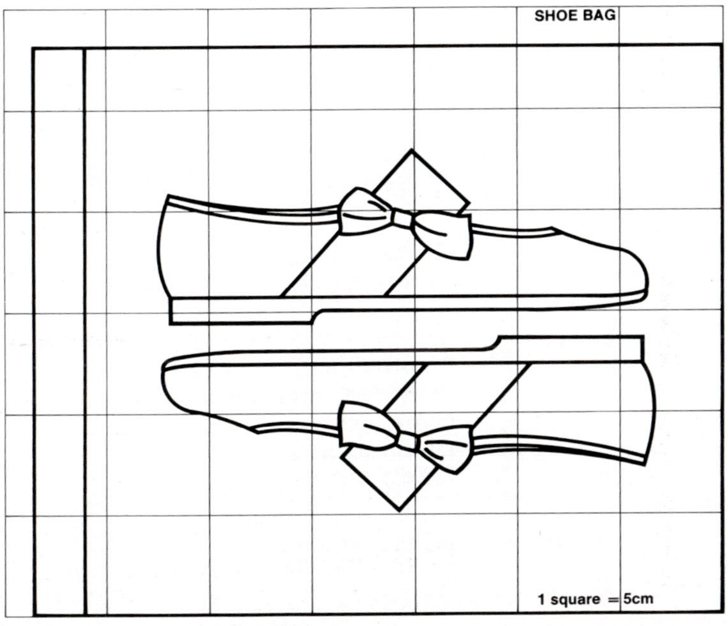

◁ LINGERIE BAG

50cm satin fabric
30cm Velcro
10cm narrow ribbon

Cut one piece fabric 40cm x 27cm and one piece fabric 36cm x 27cm.

Enlarge design from pattern on page 113. Position design as desired on larger piece of fabric. Machine stitch design with contrast thread using satin stitch (close zigzag). Trim with bow.

Turn back 3cm along one narrow edge of larger piece of fabric, so right sides are together. Baste edges in place to form a hem. Position Velcro along hem on wrong side of bag, machine stitch in place.

Turn in small hem towards right side of smaller piece of fabric on one narrow edge and position Velcro on right side of bag. Machine stitch in place. Turn Velcro section on large piece over to the right side. With right sides together, stitch fabric pieces together at sides to form bag. A pillowcase style opening will form. Turn out through Velcro opening.

SHOE BAG ▽

40cm cotton fabric
Small amount contrasting fabric
1m thin cord

Cut two pieces fabric 40cm x 30cm, or desired size. Enlarge design for shoes from diagram on page 113 and machine satin stitch design.

Cut bows from contrasting fabric (use diagram on page 113 or devise your own design). Machine satin stitch around bows and hand stitch to shoes.

Sew fabric pieces together around sides and one end leaving opening at top for casing. Form casing by turning a narrow edge then turn down 1.5cm and stitch, leaving gap for cord. Thread cord through, tie off cord ends and pull up.

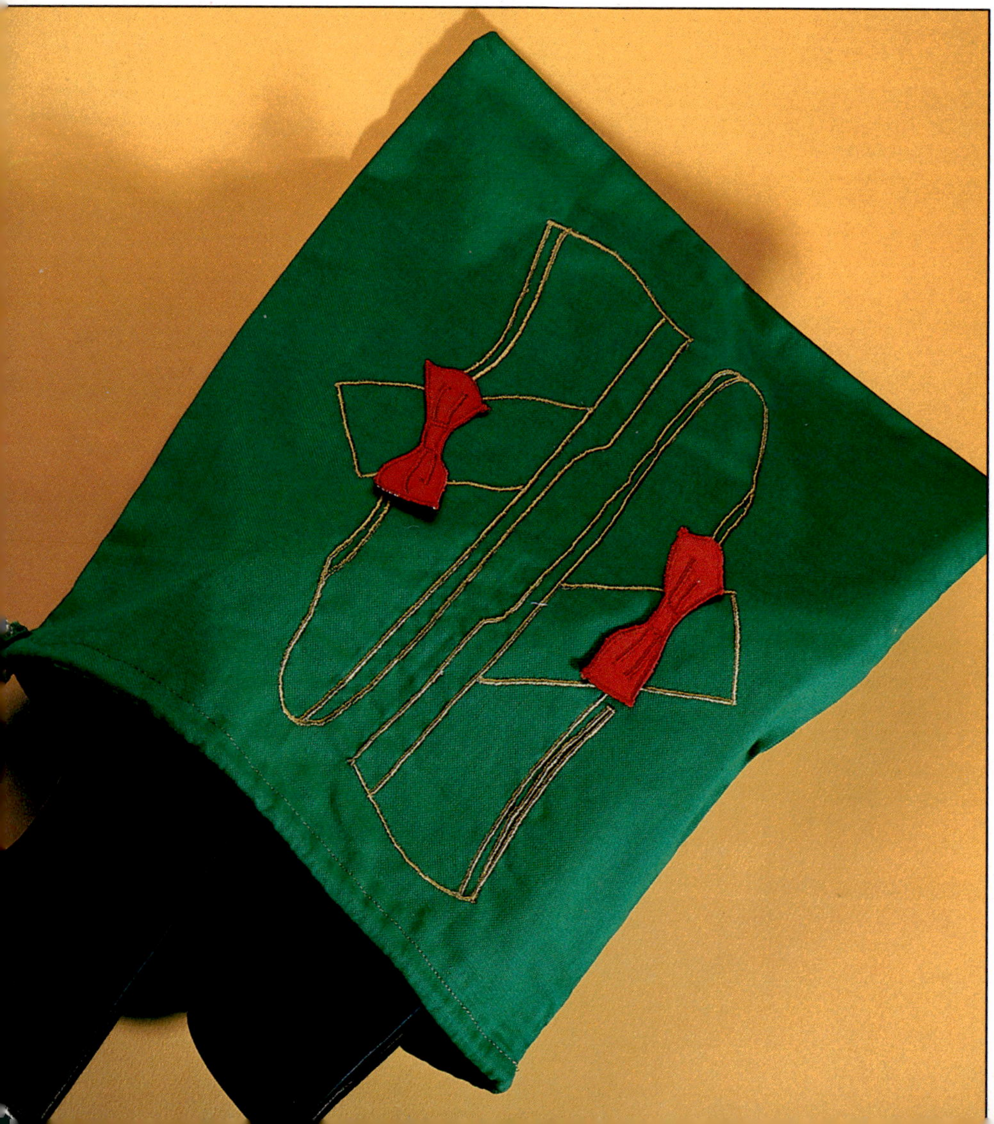

Happy Face badges by Christine Woodhead

HAPPY FACES △

Small amounts lightweight fabric
Stranded embroidery thread
29mm self cover buttons
Heavy plastic
Safety pins

Trace and embroider face on fabric using a single strand of thread. Work in back stitch and fill eyes in

with satin stitch. See page 126 for stitch instructions. Cut off stem of button so that it does not extend beyond button. Follow package directions to cover button.

Cut out circle of plastic to cover back of button. Cut out piece of fabric to cover plastic allowing an edge for turning under. Sew a small safety pin to centre of fabric. Glue fabric to plastic and turn under raw edges. Glue button and covered plastic sections together.

RIBBON ROSE BUTTONS

Small amount fabric
30mm self cover buttons
1m pink silk embroidery ribbon
Small amount green silk ribbon
Stranded embroidery thread

Use running stitch to outline button area on fabric. Work design in centre of running stitch circle following diagram on page opposite. See page 126 for stitch instructions.

The large centre flowers are woven over spokes of five straight stitches. Work five straight stitches in stranded thread then weave pink silk ribbon over and under each stitch until straight stitches are covered.

The leaves are worked in open chain by working one chain stitch either side of flower using green silk ribbon. The small flowers are French knots ; work three knots either side of button. The small leaves are worked in straight stitch; work two stitches near the French knots.

Use two strands of thread to embroider the French knots and straight stitches.

Cover buttons following manufacturer's instructions.

All buttons by students of Dover Heights College of TAFE (Commercial Needlecraft)

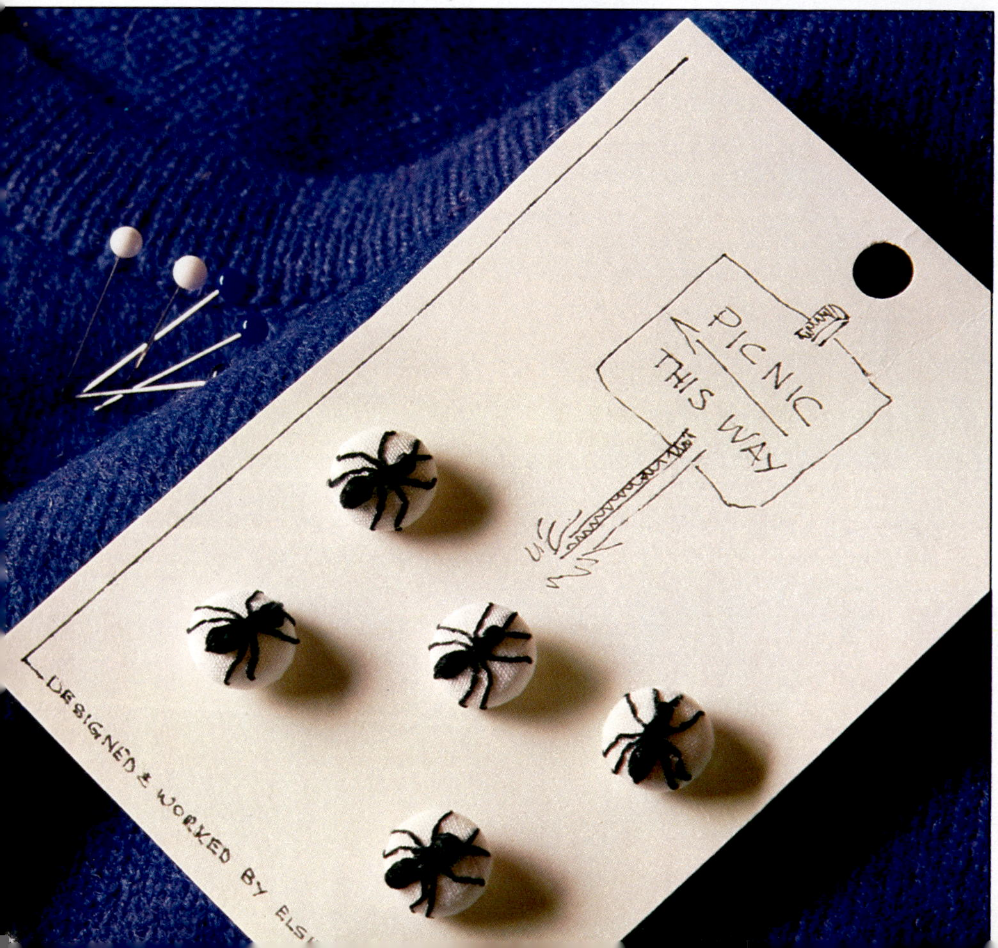

ANT BUTTONS

Small amount fabric
10mm self cover buttons
Black stranded embroidery thread

Use running stitch to outline button area on fabric. Work design opposite in running stitch circle. See page 126 for stitch instructions.

The head is a French knot made from four turns using two strands thread. The legs are worked in back stitch using one strand thread, the upper body in straight stitch, three very close stitches using two strands of thread.

The abdomen is worked in chain stitch encasing two French knots, the top knot has three turns and the bottom two turns. The abdomen is worked using two strands thread.

Cut circles of fabric and cover buttons following manufacturer's instructions.

Jumpers on both pages by Weiss Pringle

BLACK AND GOLD BEADED BUTTONS ▷

Small amount fabric
20mm self cover buttons
Gold metallic thread
Gold seed beads

Use running stitch to outline button area on fabric. In each running stitch circle, work parallel rows of stem stitch in gold thread following diagram below. See page 126 for stitch instructions.

Stitch the gold seed beads through the centre of each circle, in a line in the opposite direction to the rows of stem stitch.

Cover buttons following manufacturer's instructions.

BEETLE BUTTONS ▷

Small amount linen fabric
10mm self cover buttons
Stranded embroidery thread

Outline button area with running stitch. Work design below in centre of running stitch circle.

The body is worked in bright colours using satin stitch. See page 126 for stitch instructions. Use three strands of thread for body.

To make eyes, work two French knots at top of body using two strands of black thread. The legs and antennae are worked with a single strand of black thread in straight stitch.

Cut fabric and cover buttons following manufacturer's instructions.

ROSE BUTTONS ▷

Small amount fabric
15mm self cover buttons
Stranded embroidery thread

Use running stitch to outline button area on fabric. Work grub roses in bullion stitch as diagram at left in centre of running stitch circle. See page 126 for stitch instructions.

Work roses using three strands of thread, work dots as French knots using three strands of thread and work stems and leaves in bullion stitch using three strands of thread.

Cut fabric circles for buttons and cover them following manufacturer's instructions.

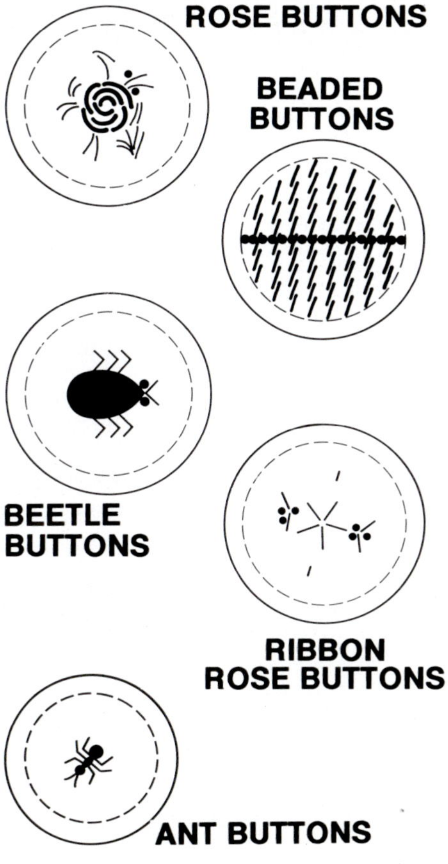

For CHRISTMAS

Handmade decorations have so much more Christmas spirit than the store bought variety! In our collection we have tree trims, stockings, a welcome wreath and bright table ware. Some are no-sew; all are easy and inexpensive to make. Use Christmas print fabrics in red and green for a traditional look or add a tinsel touch with gold and silver ribbons.

Stars by Neryl Hogan

RIGHT: Christmas Stars (instructions overpage).

Decorations by Neryl Hogan

◁ PATCHWORK BALL AND BELL

Polystyrene ball and bell
Sharp knife
Craft glue
Scraps of fabric and ribbon
Lace
Tinsel

To make patchwork bell cut four triangles fabric approximately 9cm x 6cm. Divide the bell into quarters and mark with pencil.

Push fabric into lines marked on bell with end of nail file or knife. Decorate joins with tinsel.

Make a loop of ribbon for hanging and glue in place. Decorate with a ribbon bow, if desired.

To make patchwork ball cut different sized pieces of fabric and push into ball with sharp end of nail file or knife. Form ribbon loop, attach with pin and secure with glue.

To make lace trimmed ball divide the foam ball into quarters and mark with a pencil. Cut four diamond shaped pieces fabric, approximately 10cm long and with 6cm diameter.

Push fabric into place with a knife or the end of a nail file. Glue lace along joins.

◁ CHRISTMAS STARS

For each star:
70cm x 2.5cm-wide ribbon
Craft glue
10cm narrow ribbon

Cut six pieces 2.5cm-wide ribbon into 11cm strips. Cut ends diagonally so points are both going in the same direction. See diagram below.

Fold ribbon ends together so that A and B meet to form point. Glue to secure. Glue six pieces together at sides to form star.

Cut piece narrow ribbon and double to form loop for hanging. Glue between wide ribbon sections.

To achieve patterned effect choose ribbon that is plain on one side and patterned on the other side.

CHRISTMAS BALL AND BELL ▷

Heavy cardboard
Thin wadding scrap
Fabric scrap
Glue
Lace

Trace desired shapes onto cardboard and cut out. Cut two of each shape for each decoration.

Cut wadding to fit each shape and glue on top. Cover wadding with fabric and glue to cardboard.

Attach a loop of ribbon to wrong side of one piece of cardboard and glue lace around edge of wrong side of cardboard, if desired.

Glue covered cardboard pieces together, with wrong sides facing and allow to dry before hanging.

Decorations by Neryl Hogan

Stockings by Susan Massey

◁ CHRISTMAS STOCKINGS

For each stocking:
30cm x 60cm fabric (stocking leg)
15cm x 60cm contrast fabric
30cm lace

Cut two stocking legs A from main fabric and cut four stocking cuffs B from contrast fabric. See diagram below. (Two of these will be used as the facing.)

With right sides together join stocking legs A, leaving top open. Turn out. With right sides together sew two stocking cuffs B together at sides, turn out.

With right sides together join top of A to B to form stocking. Make a loop for hanging stocking from a scrap of fabric. With right sides together, stitch facing B to top of stocking cuff B stitching loop in place at side of stocking at the same time. Hem bottom of facing, turn inside and stitch in place.

Decorate stocking with lace along join of A and B.

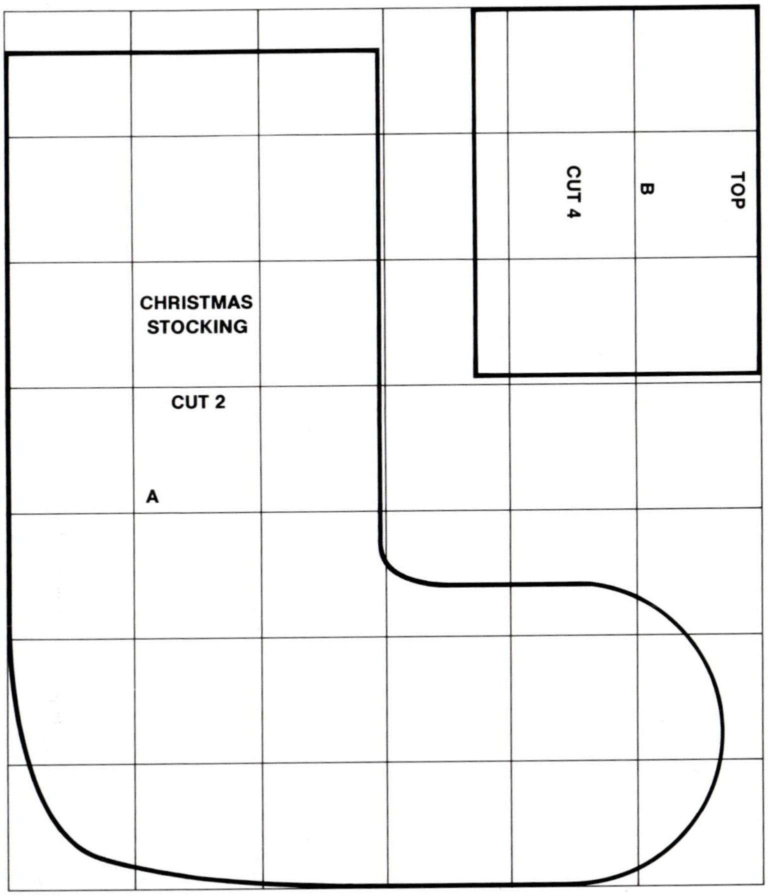

Wreath by Susan Massey

◁ CHRISTMAS WREATH

10cm of three 90cm-wide fabrics (Christmas co-ordinates)
Polyester fibre fill
1m red ribbon
1m green ribbon
2 bells
70cm wire

Cut four pieces fabric 8.5cm x 16.5cm from each of three colours or prints.

With right sides together, join narrowest sides together with 1cm seam, making fabric cylinder. Run gathering stitch around top and bottom edges of cylinder, hemming at the same time. Draw in gathers on one side, fill with polyester fibre fill, then draw in gathering on other end. Continue to do this with each piece of fabric, making 12 puffed cylinders in total. Thread them on to wire, alternating the colours.

Bend wire to form a circle and twist ends together making a loop for hanging. Cover loop with ribbon and decorate wreath with ribbon and bells.

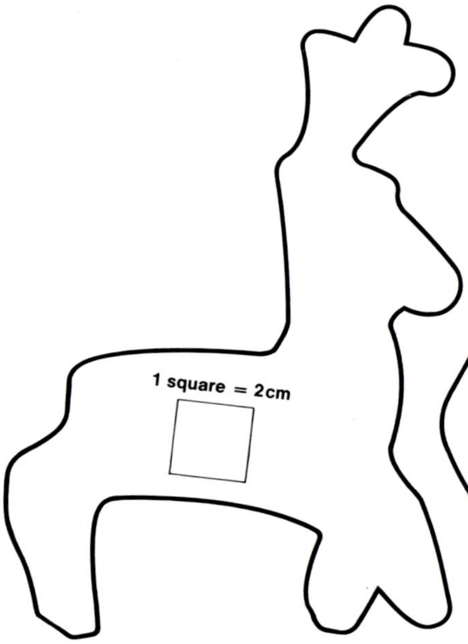

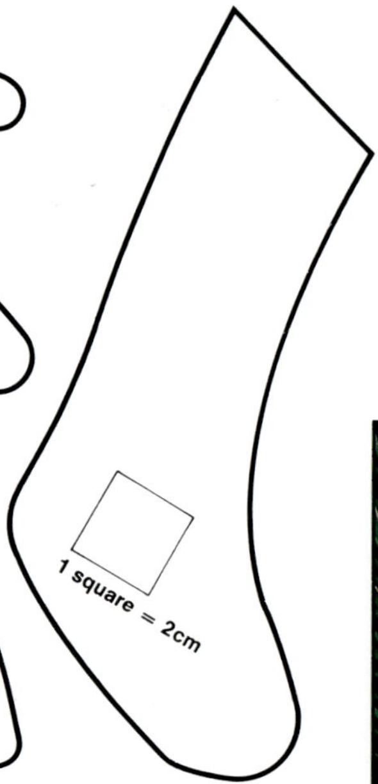

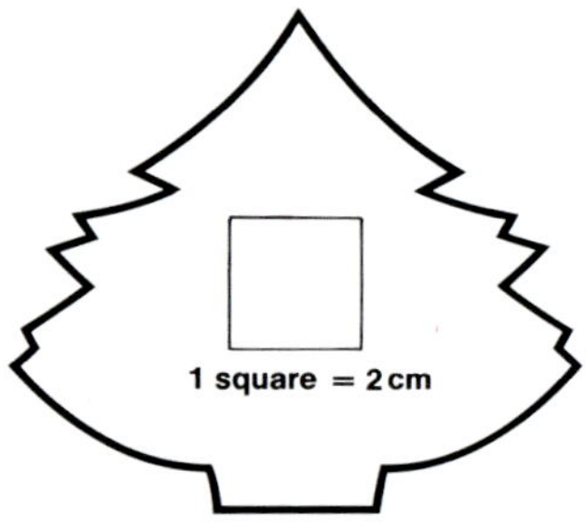

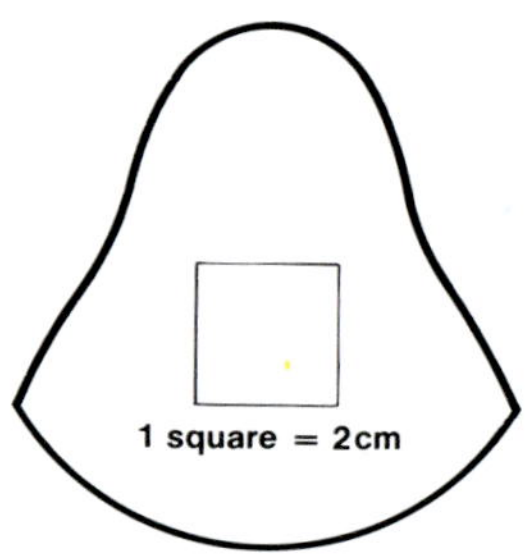

FELT DECORATIONS ▷

Felt squares
Polyester fibre fill
1m x 3mm satin ribbon
Needle with large eye

Cut felt shapes using outlines above. Cut two shapes for each decoration.

Place small amount polyester fibre fill between shapes and stitch around edges using satin ribbon. Form ribbon loop at top of decoration, for hanging.

Napkins, placemats and rings by Susan Massey

NAPKIN RINGS △

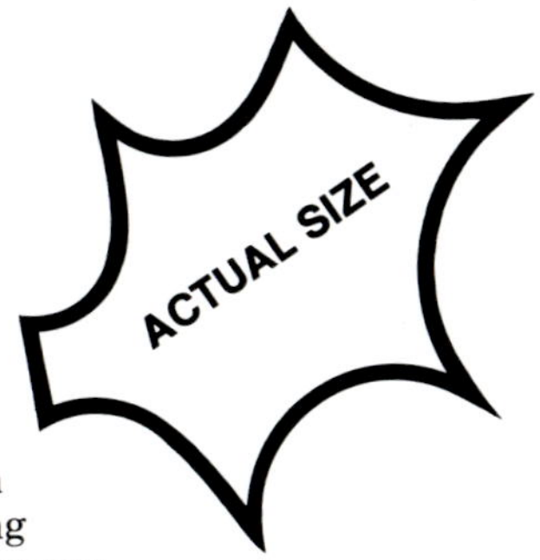

Small quantity red fabric
Heavy fusible interfacing
Green felt
Red beads
Craft glue

Cut two rectangles fabric 18cm x 5cm. Cut one piece interfacing same size as fabric, attach to wrong side of one piece fabric.

With right sides together join two strips fabric with 1cm seams, stitching around three sides leaving one end open. Turn right side out, turn in seam allowance on open end and slip stitch ends together to form a ring.

Cut two holly leaves from felt. See diagram above. Attach these and two beads to napkin ring with craft glue. Reinforce with stitching, if desired.

Instructions for placemats and napkins overpage.

Reindeer by Neryl Hogan

◁PEG REINDEER

3 wooden clip pegs
Scraps of felt
Braid
2 small eyes
Craft glue

Glue two pegs together side by side. Glue third peg on the front about one-third the way down. See diagram below.

Cut 2.5cm square felt for blanket, trim with braid and glue over two body pegs.

Attach piece cord or ribbon for tail then join back edges of felt blanket together.

Cut another small piece felt for hat and glue on to third peg just above face. Glue eyes in place.

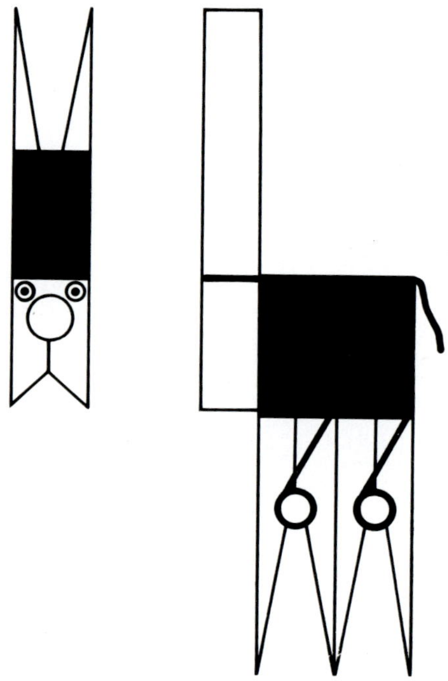

◁NAPKINS

For two napkins:
40cm x 90cm fabric

For each napkin cut 36cm square of fabric (or larger if desired).

Turn under and machine a small hem on all sides of square.

◁REVERSIBLE PLACEMATS

For two placemats:
30cm x 90cm red print fabric
30cm x 90cm green fabric
Bias binding

For each placemat cut one oval shape in each colour fabric. See diagram at right.

Place ovals wrong sides together and stitch bias binding around edges, overlapping ends of bias.

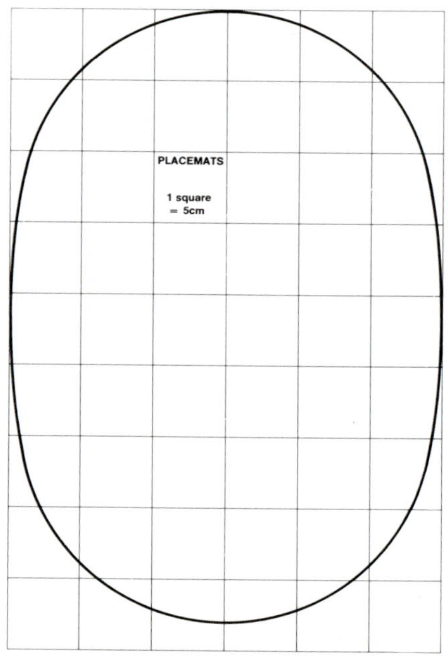

ABBREVIATIONS

KNITTING AND CROCHET ABBREVIATIONS

K = knit; **P** = purl; **sl** = slip; **psso** = pass slipped stitch(es) over; **tbl** = through back of loop(s); **y bk** = yarn back — take yarn under needle from purling position into knitting position; **y ft** = yarn front — bring yarn under needle from knitting position into purling position; **y fwd** = yarn forward — bring yarn under needle, then over into knitting position again, thus making a stitch; **yon** = yarn over needle — take yarn over top of needle into knitting position, thus making a stitch; **yrn** = yarn round needle — take yarn right around needle into purling position, thus making a stitch; **"M1"** = make 1 — pick up loop which lies before next stitch, place on left-hand needle and knit (or purl) into back of loop; **garter st** = every row knit; **stocking st** = 1 row knit, 1 row purl; **reverse stocking st** = 1 row purl, 1 row knit (purl side is right side).

When instructions read — "Cast off 2 sts, K2" (or similar stitches), the stitch left on the right-hand needle, after casting off, is counted as one stitch.

ch = chain; **sp** = space; **sl st** = slip stitch; **dc** = double crochet; **yoh** = yarn over hook; **h tr** = half treble — pass yarn round hook, draw a loop through next stitch, draw a loop through all 3 loops on hook; **tr** = treble — pass yarn round hook, draw a loop through next stitch, draw a loop through first 2 loops on hook, then draw another loop through 2 remaining loops; **d tr** = double treble — pass yarn twice round hook, draw a loop through next stitch, draw a loop through first 2 loops on hook, draw a loop through next 2 loops, then another through last 2 loops; **t tr** = triple treble — pass yarn three times round hook, draw a loop through next stitch, draw a loop through first 2 loops on hook, draw a loop through next 2 loops, another through next 2 loops, then another through last 2 loops.

alt = alternate; **beg** = begin or beginning; **cont** = continue; **dec** = decrease, decreased, decreases or decreasing; **foll** = following or follows; **inc** = increase, increased, increases or increasing; **incl** = including or inclusive; **0** = no rows, stitches or times; **patt** = pattern; **rem** = remain, remains, remainder or remaining; **rep** = repeat; **st, sts** = stitch, stitches; **tog** = together; **cm** = centimetre(s); **mm** = millimetre(s); **ins** = inches.

The first row is always the right side of the work unless otherwise stated.

ENLARGING

ENLARGING USING A PHOTOCOPY MACHINE

All diagrams can be easily enlarged using a photocopy machine. Photocopy the diagram with machine set for enlarging, until the squares on the enlarged copy match the size stated on the grid. E.g., 1cm or 5cm.

ENLARGING USING A GRID

All the diagrams in this book can be enlarged easily using simple methods that ensure all parts remain in proportion.

METHOD 1

Some diagrams in this book show one square only on the diagram, rather than a complete grid (see animal pencil cases, page 54). To enlarge these diagrams, simply extend the square into a grid of squares the same size as the original square. Then enlarge the diagram as for method 2.

METHOD 2

Look at the diagram you want to enlarge; for example, the tropical fish on page 53. This shows a grid of squares over the image to be enlarged, with a scale of 1 square = 1cm indicated. This means that each square, when enlarged, should measure 1cm by 1cm.

On a separate piece of paper, rule a bigger grid of 1cm squares to make the actual size pattern.

Carefully copy the small diagram onto the large grid one square at a time.

Copy all squares, checking the work as you go, until the actual size pattern is completed.

Note. In this case the small squares represent larger ones 1cm by 1cm. However, the small squares can represent any measurement the designer indicates, such as 5cm or 10cm.

METHOD 3

This method lets you enlarge a design to any size you want, instead of following the designer's idea. If you want to enlarge a motif to suit a cushion, but don't know how to copy it accurately — this method breaks the design into very small components.

1. First draw a rectangle (or square) around the small design. Rule a diagonal line from bottom left corner to top right corner, then rule another line from bottom right corner to top left corner. The centre is where they cross each other.

1

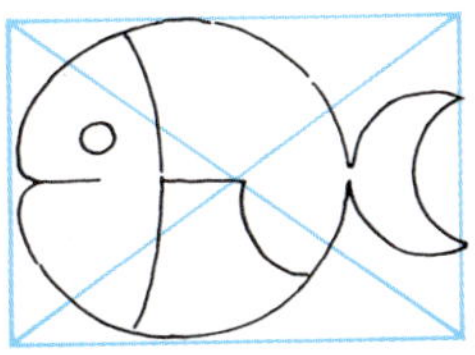

2. Now rule a vertical line from the mid-point of the top line to the mid-point of the bottom line. Rule a horizontal line from the mid-point of the left side to the mid-point of the right side.

2

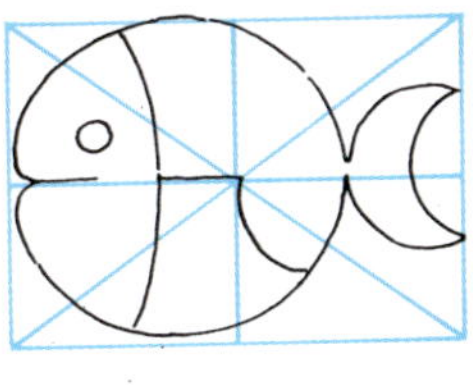

3. Rule a "diamond" from mid-point on the bottom line to mid-point of right side, to mid-point of top line; to mid-point of left side, to mid-point of bottom line.

3

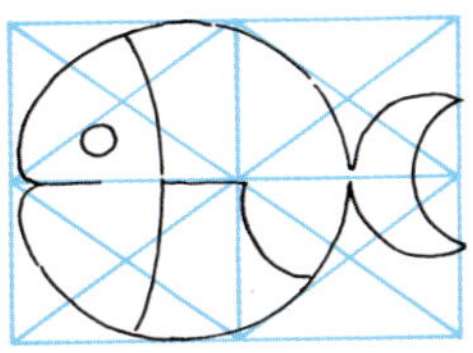

4. Rule a horizontal line across the centre of each small square, then rule a vertical line down the centre of each small rectangle.

4

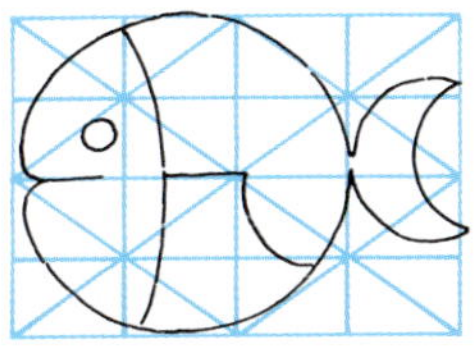

5. On a separate piece of paper, rule a bigger grid the same way to the size required for the finished design. Copy original design from small divisions into larger divisions.

5

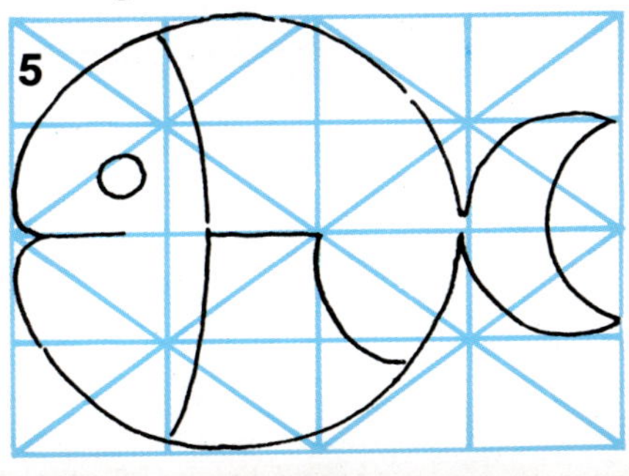

STITCHES

BULLION STITCH OR GRUB ROSE

BULLION STITCH OR GRUB ROSE

Bring needle up at A, down at B and up at A again, leaving needle in fabric. Wind thread around needle point 6 to 8 times. Pull needle through fabric and thread, keeping thread twists in place. Position twists toward B and insert needle. Arrange a group of bullion stitches to make a grub rose.

PADDED SATIN STITCH

Work split stitches around outline. Work satin stitches across the shape. Work top satin stitch layer in the desired direction.

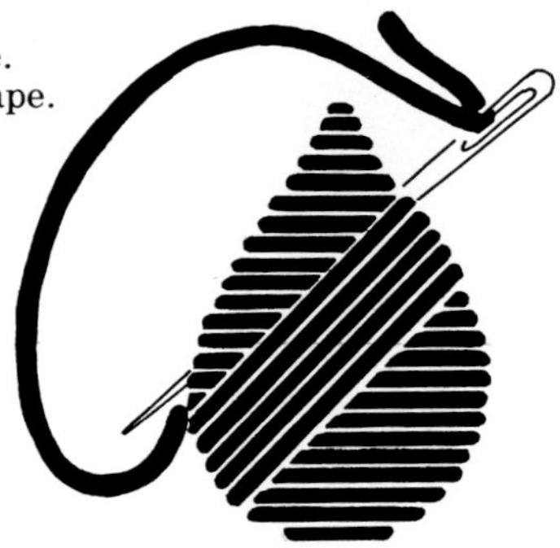

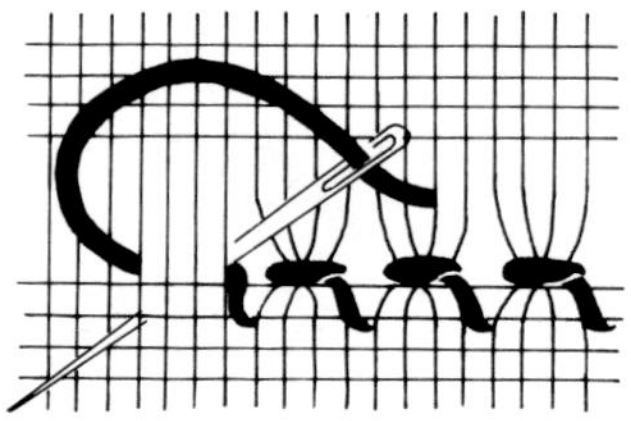

HEM STITCH

Draw out the required number of threads. Bring working thread out two threads down from drawn threads. Take needle behind four threads, then around same four threads, coming out two threads down.

LONG & SHORT SATIN STITCH

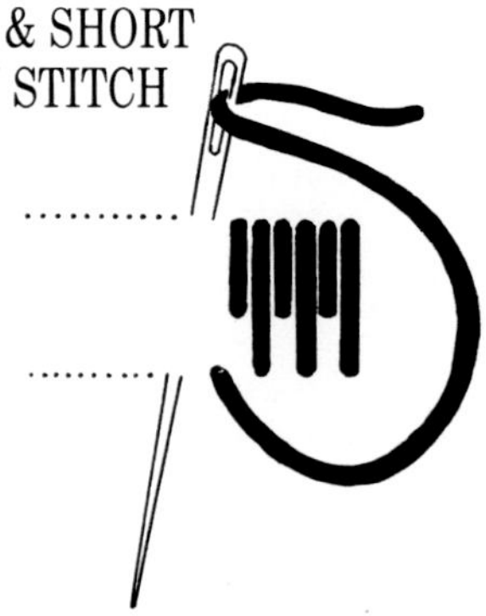

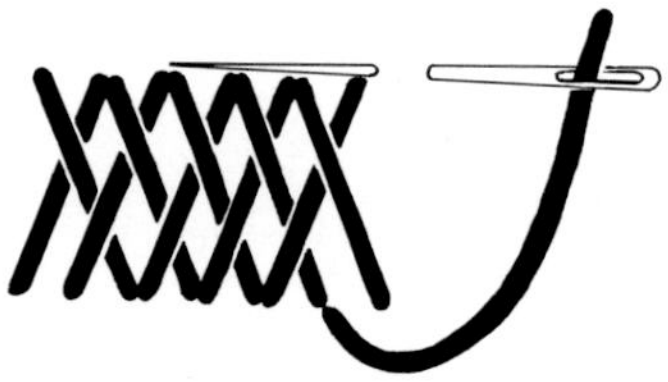

SHADOW WORK

Work this closed herringbone stitch on fine fabric from wrong side. Small stitches show on the right side and thread colour shows through fabric, to create shadow work.

KNITTING STITCH

Bring the needle up at bottom of knit stitch and around base of stitch above. Take needle under top of stitch below, keeping yarn same tension as knitting.

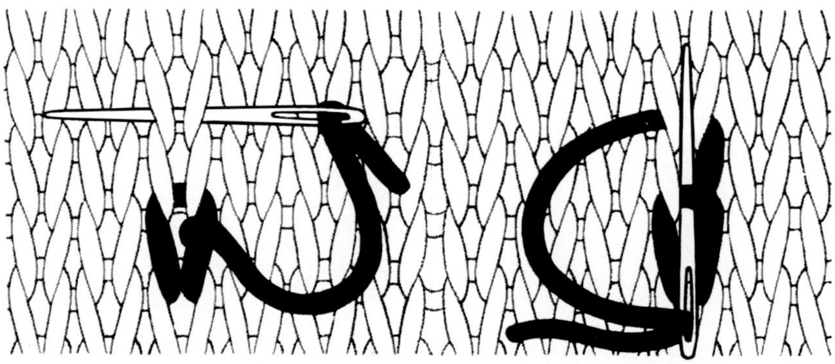

CROSS STITCH

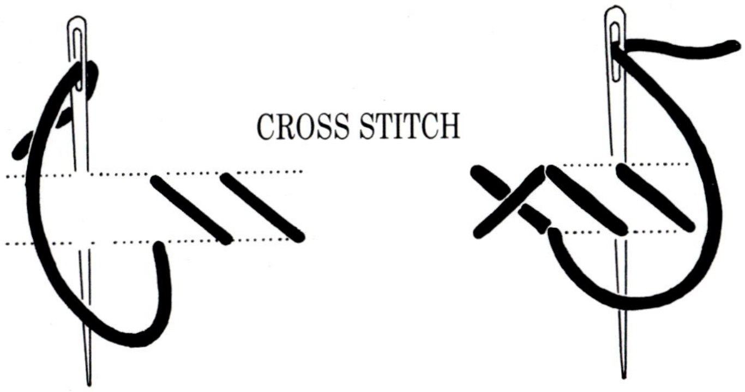

FRENCH KNOT

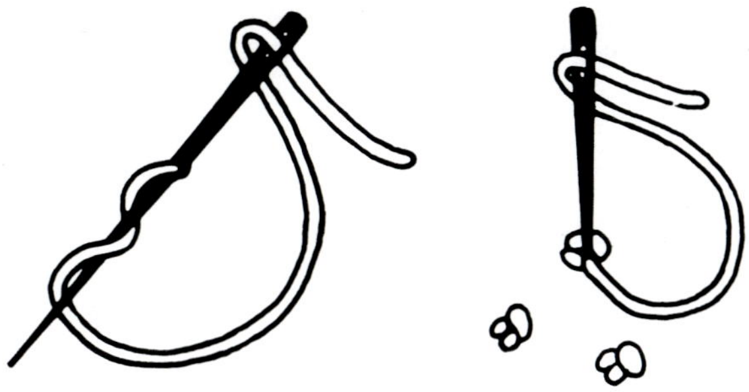

SATIN STITCH

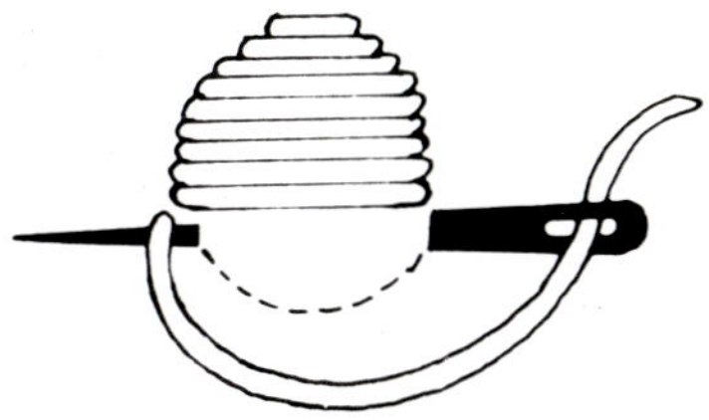

CHAIN STITCH

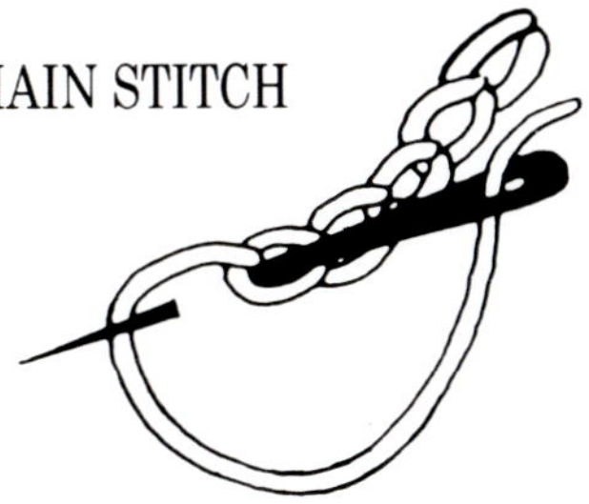

RUNNING STITCH

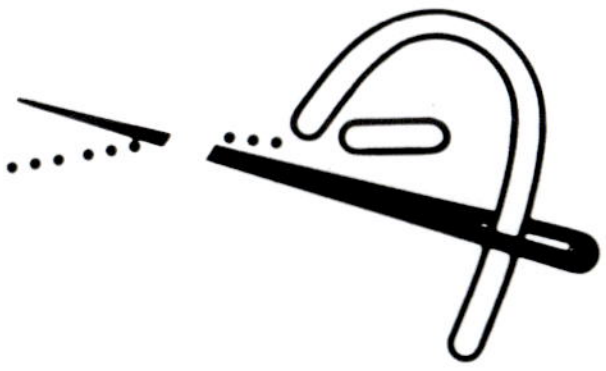

STRAIGHT STITCH

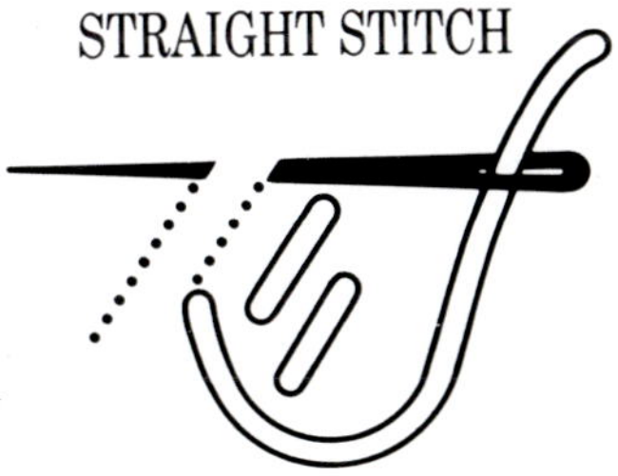

BACK STITCH

STEM STITCH

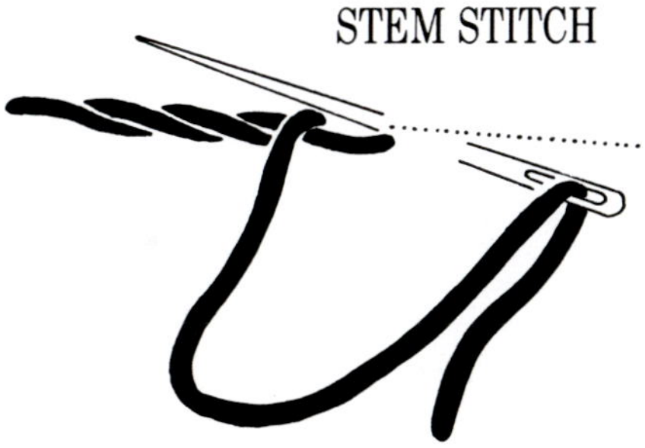

RIBBON ROSES

1. Fold ribbon at a 90 degree angle in the centre of the ribbon length.

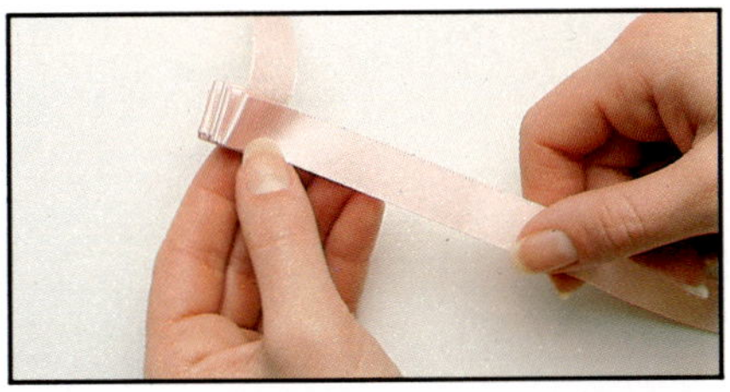

3. Continue folding the ends of the ribbon back and forth, alternating the ends being folded. Make about 20 folds.

5. With one hand at the base of the folded section, pull the other end of the ribbon down to form the rose.

2. Fold ribbon back across first fold.

4. Hold the ends of the ribbon and release the folded section.

6. Tie off the base of the rose. Ends can be trimmed and the rose stitched in place.

INDEX